CREDIT MANAGEMENT FOR PROPERTY PROFESSIONALS

The Fine Art of Not Losing Money

by

Duncan Grubb

Grosvenor House
Publishing Limited

This book is published by
Grosvenor House Publishing Ltd
Link House
140 The Broadway, Tolworth, Surrey, Kt6 7Ht.
www.grosvenorhousepublishing.co.uk

A CIP record for this book
is available from the British Library

ISBN 978-1-78623-744-6

Dedicated to my Wife, Children, and to all those enlightened colleagues who, during the course of my career, have followed my advice.

Author's Note

The information contained within this book relates exclusively to the UK commercial property sector, where businesses let property to other businesses, irrespective of whether the tenants themselves are individuals, partnerships, companies or charities.

This book is not intended for use within the residential property sector, where private homes and personal possessions are involved, and where social sensitivities dictate that a different approach to the landlord and tenant relationship is required.

Table of Contents

Introduction

This is not intended to be a text book, nor is it supposed to be the last word on "how to avoid not getting paid by your tenants". Instead what I'm hoping to provide is a simple set of touch points and no go areas to enable you to avoid the pitfalls that so many people encounter when conducting business in good faith with others. In my thirty plus years in the credit industry, much of it in property, I've come across most of the situations that can crop up to disrupt the landlord and tenant relationship, and I'd like to share my thoughts and experiences with you a) for the good of all, b) for my own professional satisfaction, and c) so that the unscrupulous people who play the system don't get away with it again!

If this sounds like I become emotionally involved in these situations don't be misled – I don't. I do however regard them as competitive events, where a bit of healthy determination to win can give you an edge and make all the difference. I've never been remotely interested in gambling purely because I don't like losing, and I'm convinced that this attitude has helped me in my career. No one sets out to be unsuccessful, and all we are asking for as Credit Professionals is payment of agreed amounts of money from our contractual counterparties on the day they are due - no more and no less.

I should stress that there are always situations where genuine hardship or unforeseen circumstances can affect a tenant's ability to honour their financial obligations to the landlord, but hopefully the following sections will help you to identify the instances where leniency is justified and a softer approach required. In general practice however, if somebody owes you money and has it, he'll pay you - the problems arise when he either hasn't got it, or didn't owe it to you in the first place.

Consistency of course is everything, so whatever set of rules you choose to establish must be universally applied. This will prevent accusations of favouritism or persecution and hopefully avoid the dead rat in the post at Christmas time.

I do hope you find the following pages useful.

A Process not a Remedy

The Credit industry's ongoing attempt to legitimise itself and improve the status of Credit Professionals on the management teams of businesses has still only met with limited success. Granted that most modern companies now accept that getting paid on time is not a given, and that credit control will always cost some money; many still fail to see the financial and administrative benefits of spending a relatively small amount on prevention, and continue to waste a fortune making unnecessary mistakes.

Credit management is all too often an afterthought, and many businesses continue to adopt a strategy of revenue maximisation at all costs, paying little attention to either the financial calibre of their customer base, or the negative effect of payment default on their own business.

This attitude is particularly prevalent in the property sector, where surveyors often have total control of a project from its inception to delivery, and where the financial evaluation of the counterparty is neither within their comfort zone, nor a primary objective.

The traditional set up of a property company gives the asset manager / surveyor pretty much total control of the operation of his or her property (whether it is a shopping centre, a retail park, or an office block), with the credit control team being a back of shop support facility with little autonomy or ability to either prevent predictable problems occurring, or to deal with them once they have happened.

This setup doesn't work, and the more enlightened property companies are beginning to realise it.

Another popular misconception is that credit management and debt recovery are one and the same thing. The truth is that although they are closely connected, each is quite different from the other.

Credit management is a process, and debt recovery is a remedy.

Credit management is a set of procedures designed to prevent payment problems occurring in the first place, and debt recovery is another set of procedures for dealing with situations where credit management hasn't worked, and where payment problems need to be rectified swiftly.

We'll deal with each of these sections separately, as if you get the first one right, you won't need the other - except that you will of course, because a) we all live in the real world where accidents can and do happen, and b) there will always be someone in your organisation who thinks they know better than you do, and who takes unnecessary risks as a result.

Where do you fit in?

There is currently no standard position or authority level for a Credit Controller / Credit Manager within the hierarchy of a typical company or business; it just depends on the level of enlightenment of the senior management and the level of bad debts that the company and its stakeholders have had to deal with in the past. This all cuts both ways, as even though it can be fairly easy to make a name for yourself by making problems go away, you will always have to justify your existence in the eyes of the senior management, and we'll deal with this more fully later on in the section entitled "The Credit Controller's Curse".

Part of the authority problem is the terminology itself, as the title "Credit Controller" can cover a multitude of levels, from the Head of Credit for a FTSE 100 multinational to the book keeper of a small operation, who manages to chase a few cheques once he or she has finished the payroll. This is not meant to over inflate the value of one individual in this example or diminish that of the other - they are both very important, but it does demonstrate how the status of the Credit Controller can vary depending on the circumstances, often leading to the contribution that a full time Credit Professional can make to the wider business being overlooked and undervalued.

This situation is unlikely to change in the short term, firstly due to the different skill levels required in the previous examples, but more importantly because there are currently no professional barriers to entry. The CICM qualification system is a giant step in the right direction, however many employers do not insist on this professional qualification as a primary requirement as they would with a candidate from an alternative profession (this can lead to a bit of snobbery from members of other professional organisations as well).

Personally I would like to see a Credit Management module in every business studies syllabus, and am still amazed that debt collection and revenue stream management is so often absent from such courses, when every other element of running and managing a business is examined in micro detail.

The successful Credit Professional (and let's not be coy about what we call ourselves), will have established his or her position in the workflow before a deal is done and not after, demonstrating the additional safety factor and financial comfort available to the business from a proper evaluation of the financial status of the customer base. This can be undertaken a) by the Credit Professional individually, b) by accepting the recommended credit limits of established credit reporting agencies such as Experian or Dun & Bradstreet, or by a combination of the two. Ultimately it doesn't matter which method is used, as either way the risks are set out for all to see, and the company's Leasing Team will be able to concentrate on tenants who can afford to pay the proposed levels of rent, and avoid those that cannot.

In too many cases Surveyors still regard themselves as the sole owners of the company's properties, viewing the Credit Team as support staff with no autonomy, and there to be drafted in only once a problem has occurred. This is an old fashioned, misguided view for the reasons I've already mentioned, and however important the Surveyor / Asset Manager's role as an ambassador for his company, he is (and this will hurt some of them a bit) merely a front man for a much wider relationship between landlord and tenant.

In reality a good Credit Controller will interact with tenants just as much as the Asset Management Team. This ranges from the initial financial evaluation and ongoing monitoring (ideally with face to face meetings), all the way through to debt recovery and litigation where necessary. Indeed a "courtesy" call from the Credit Controller to a tenant's Property Director, flagging a payment problem and explaining that recovery action is about to be taken, can often resolve things quite speedily in my experience.

We all live in a changing commercial climate and problems do arise in spite of everybody's best intentions, but if credit terms do need to be reviewed, it's imperative that negotiations involve the Credit Team, otherwise what's the point in escalating a problem from Credit Controller to Credit Manager - both Credit Professionals, for it then to be handed over to a member of the surveying team - with no credit experience and a very different agenda, to renegotiate the entire deal. Ideally if a third party (such as a Key Account Manager) wishes to get involved in a credit issue then it should be to enforce a Credit Control decision, not to renegotiate or undermine it.

It is therefore important to quickly gain acceptance through success, and in so doing bolster your position in the company's hierarchy – remember, they all think they can do without you and would rather not have to involve you in the decision making process. Your suggested changes to internal procedures will undoubtedly raise a few hackles, but it's then your job to demonstrate how they add value to the business and make tenant default a rarity.

There is a myth that Surveyors don't understand finance – it's partly true, but they're usually pretty clued up on rental income, arrears, and the effect of insolvent tenants on their forecasts, so if you can help maximise "safe" income, minimise arrears, and sidestep deals with tenants who are likely to go bust in the near future, they'll all suddenly want to be your friend – particularly if their bonuses depend on the achievement of financial targets.

The Commercial
Property Landscape

Commercial landlords are quite different from other suppliers in that they have a contractual and far more interlocked relationship with their customers - or tenants as we sometimes call them. The main difference is the inability to terminate supply without a Court order, unlike a commercial wholesaler, who will simply stop sending any more T-shirts until the bill for the last shipment has been settled.

Incidentally the definition of "supplier" is entirely appropriate for the landlord, as he is providing the tenant with space in which to conduct his business, and in exchange for which he receives payment of rent and other charges falling due under the terms of the contract or lease. In situations where the relationship between the parties becomes more complicated, for instance when the landlord is asked to forego income in order to assist a struggling tenant in one of his centres, it often helps to remember that the reason the landlord exists is to supply space, to be paid for it, and to make money for his investors.

It's also important to periodically remind tenants exactly what kind of organisation their landlord is. The popular view of a large landlord as a fat cat institution which, having built a property, just sits back and collects the rent with little or no involvement in day to day operations couldn't be further from the truth. In fact nine out of ten commercial landlords are investment companies which just happen to deal in property, and whose investors expect to see a return on their money otherwise they'll pretty quickly move it somewhere else. Tenants often don't (or choose not to) see the amount of active management undertaken by the landlord in terms of facilities and security, and in the case of retail properties, demographic and catchment area analyses and marketing initiatives all designed to maximise footfall and drive sales for the tenants, The fact that the landlord is a business in its own right and not some form of benevolent uncle which can forego rent without any negative impact can be a bit of a shock to some tenants, but the sooner and more often the point is made the better.

A tenant will expect to be paid the sticker price for its merchandise and will look aghast if a customer attempts to haggle, so why is it acceptable for tenants to expect rent concessions from landlords as soon as things start to get difficult? Before you say it I know that shops lower their prices during sales, but it's not the same situation as sale prices are part of the original offer and acceptance agreement between supplier and customer, whereas rental payments relate to an agreement which is already in place, and which stipulates the amounts of money to be paid to the landlord and the dates on which they are due.

Now if you're beginning to think that you should view the landlord / tenant relationship as if it is between a finance company and a borrower, or a building society and a mortgagee rather than a customer and supplier, then you are absolutely right and once you adopt that that mind-set, then everything else you need to do to manage that relationship and ensure compliance falls into place and seems entirely logical.

The Contract

Who is it with?

The tenancy agreement can take a number of forms ranging from Landlord & Tenant Act leases, Outside Act leases (where both parties agree in advance that the obligations on both parties contained within the Act will not apply), to agreements to lease, licences to occupy, and tenancies at will. We'll assume that all of these require payment to the landlord of some kind whether it's base rent, turnover rent, service charges, insurance and water charges or even possibly rates. Ultimately it makes no difference as the requirement to pay the landlord money at certain times is a common factor, but it's amazing that the most common error landlords make, is not knowing who their tenants actually are.

It is so often the case that a Letting Agent will refer to a tenant by their brand or trade name when proposing a deal to the landlord, and the landlord does the same thing when processing the paperwork internally. Once the lawyers get involved the precise identity of the company or entity taking the space will usually be bottomed out, but at that point it's too late to do any proper due diligence on the financial status of the proposed tenant and their covenant strength. The lawyers will assume that the tenant has approved the deal having had sight of all the relevant information, but that's often not the case, and the first time anybody realises anything is wrong is when action has to be taken to enforce payment or another breach of lease obligations. Suddenly the top notch brand proves to be only a small independent retailer operating under a franchise agreement with the main trading company.

A newly appointed Credit Manager should therefore examine the tenant database and confirm exactly who is occupying the properties as quickly as possible, not only to find out who to send legal documents to, but to get an overall impression of the financial stability of the tenant base and identify any weaknesses. Letting Agents and Surveyors make rotten Credit Controllers, so don't leave this part of the business to them, but insist that the correct legal entity – whether it is a limited company, limited liability partnership, public limited company or proprietorship, is correctly identified on the lease proposal and the financial assessment conducted accordingly. Just ask yourself "who do I sue if it all goes wrong?"

You might think this is all blindingly obvious, but to assume that the "Smiths" on the database means W.H. Smith Plc is asking for trouble as there are a large number of companies within the W.H. Smith Group as it is, and even more unrelated companies with the word Smith in their names.

I repeat, this is the most common mistake made by landlords and it's the Credit Manager's job to make sure that it doesn't happen by ensuring the landlord's tenant database includes the following:-

1. The correct legal entity - either the correct company details of the principal tenant (including the registration number) or the name of the individual(s) if you are dealing with a proprietorship or partnership. A trade name or firm name will not do.

2. The registered office address of the company or the home address in the case of a proprietorship or partnership (all partners' addresses required). These must be verified by:-

3. A credit check by an agency such as Dun & Bradstreet or Experian for companies, and Callcredit or Experian for individuals. You get what you pay for with these service providers, and although some of the smaller operators will be able to provide cheaper information, you need to check how current it is as some firms only update their information weekly to save money.

These requirements apply not only to tenants, but guarantors and sureties under the lease as well (see section "The Tenant").

The term

It's often overlooked, but how long will your relationship with the tenant last? The longer the lease term, the more chance there is of payment default. This could be caused by changes in the financial status of the tenant over time, brand or technical obsolescence, demographic changes affecting the customer base and/or the willingness to visit the property (particularly if it's a retail unit relying on footfall). It's also important to look at the health and lease terms of the surrounding units in a retail centre as even if the tenant in question is riding high in popularity, it could be surrounded by dark units or failing businesses at some point and nobody will want to go there.

We'll come onto tenant covenant evaluation a bit later, but in general the longer the lease, the better the financials of the proposed tenant will need to be. I know some will say that things can go up as well as down and that some tenants will become more successful as time goes by. I agree – jolly good luck to them – but as this scenario doesn't present the Credit Manager with a problem, it's of little consequence other than a) in the impact it has on the trading of the adjacent units as I've already mentioned, and b) the desirability of doing more deals with this good quality tenant in other locations within the landlord's portfolio.

Coming back to our building society / finance company analogy, in such cases the term of the arrangement is a crucial part of the deal, and I'm always surprised how little importance landlords attach to it.

Break Clauses

Landlord breaks

A landlord break can be a valuable credit management tool – provided the tenant doesn't want to leave of course – as it allows the landlord to end the relationship with the tenant at a certain point in time if he so chooses. The break also shortens the term of the landlord & tenant relationship, and can therefore be inserted into a deal where the long term financial stability of a prospective tenant is questionable.

The threat of eviction from a unit which is making a good profit will certainly concentrate the tenant's mind when it comes to settling the rents on time. As even if the break date hasn't yet arrived, the landlord will be taking past payment performance into account along with the other operational and strategic factors surrounding the decision to either keep the tenant in and trading, or to exercise the break.

A rolling landlord only break clause without a specific break date is clearly the best option for debt recovery purposes, however there will be no incentive for the tenant to invest in the fabric of the unit if he can be booted out at a month's notice, so it's a case of swings and roundabouts with one of these.

Tenant breaks

Tenant break clauses are usually seen by landlords as a bad thing, in that they negatively affect property valuations (more about that later), but if a notice to exercise a tenant break is to be deemed valid, there will usually be a condition in the lease that there must be no arrears, so at least the rent for the period in which the break date sits will be paid on time and in full.

Mutual breaks

The best and worst of both worlds, but the landlord probably wins on balance.

Trading Information

Whether rents are paid in advance in regular amounts, or in arrears based on a percentage of the turnover of the unit, or by base rent advance payments with a turnover top up adjustment in arrears later on, it's very important to obtain as much trading data from any kind of tenant which exists by selling things or providing services in exchange for money. Ideally the requirement to provide weekly or monthly sales data should be set out in the lease in order to enable the landlord to enforce it, as the tenant will be in breach if it doesn't materialise.

It's then a question of calculating the outgoings in rent, service charges and (crucially) business rates as a percentage of the money going through the till, in order to arrive at a total occupancy cost. The target figure varies from sector to sector, with fast food operators having different models to Ferrari dealerships, but in general if the total occupancy cost starts to go far above 20% of turnover that particular trading unit may be struggling to support itself.

The most important side effect of collecting trading data is the ease with which a trend analysis of total occupancy costs can be put together, showing whether a tenant is improving or declining over time compared to its sector peers, or just those in adjacent units if we're talking about a retail environment. The trend analysis will prove invaluable to the leasing and asset management teams, and will help with the financial evaluation of future deals with the same tenant which we'll come onto later in the section "The Tenant".

Things to Avoid

Mixing residential and commercial property under one lease

On 6th April 2014 the UK Government in its apparent wisdom abolished an 800 year old piece of legislation called the Law of Distress, which allowed landlords to place a possession order over goods held in a property where rent had not been paid until such time as it had, or ultimately seize the goods and send them off to auction with the proceeds going some way (but generally not very far) towards offsetting the rent arrears. The Law of Distress was always seen as a fair addition to the landlords' debt recovery procedures, as he is in the unique position of not being able to terminate supply without a court order if the tenant doesn't pay up. Other suppliers, including utilities, are not prevented from exiting a bad business relationship in this way.

The replacement for Distress is a badly thought out, under researched, bureaucratic, unworkable and hideously expensive regime called CRAR, or Commercial Rent Arrears Recovery. The instigators of the change were apparently the European Court of Human Rights (insert expletive here), who claimed that Distress had to be abolished because there was no immediate defence against having your goods seized, other than by applying for a court injunction. Their solution was to abolish distress altogether.

The Ministry of Justice claim that they have managed to "salvage" some of the landlords' rights by proposing CRAR, and that the landlord community should be eternally grateful.

As a credit professional I am paid to be cynical, and I pride myself on doing it well, and blow me down if CRAR doesn't contain all the exclusions and anti-avoidance measures that tenant groups have been lobbying the government for, for years, such as:

1. CRAR can only be invoked to collect pure rent, not service charges or insurance even if they are reserved as rent under the lease.

2. All-inclusive rents have to be apportioned to allow for the estimated rental component only, with the balance being uncollectable under CRAR.

3. A seven day notice period before goods are seized, giving unscrupulous tenants a chance to clear the unit of stock and abscond.

4. A complete ban on the use of CRAR on residential properties even if there is a commercial element.

You can probably tell that I am unimpressed with all this, but unfortunately it's now law and we have to abide by it, so for new lettings it's vital that there is a complete disconnect between residential and commercial elements of a property where the two exist side by side. In other words you need one lease showing a specific demised area for the residential part, and another for the commercial part, otherwise you will not be able to utilise CRAR as a debt recovery tool at all.

This restriction typically applies to shops with a residential flat above and where one lease covers the entire property. What it doesn't mean is that a commercial tenant can sleep on a camp bed in the store room and claim it's a residential property - it has to be specified in the lease. We can at least all be happy about that.

Turnover based break clauses

These nasty little things are sometimes included in leases by tenants who are new to an area or country, and aren't sure how well they will trade. The clause will stipulate a minimum amount of turnover required for a specific number of years, below which the tenant will have a right to break. The insertion of the clause may well be a condition of the letting and that's fine as long as the credit team are made aware of it, and can take it into account when evaluating the proposal. However it's often not flagged and only shows up when a break notice arrives out of the blue, ruining everybody's rental forecasts and making the Asset Manager worry about his bonus. Sometimes the clause will be contained in a side letter which for reasons best known to the letting team doesn't get shown to the credit team. The phrase "hit and hope" springs to mind and accurately sums up the mentality of many letting teams across the industry, although they will see things quite differently of course.

In short, all beak notices need to be reflected (along with all the other components of the letting) in the internal document which is circulated for signoff before the lawyers get involved. One of the signatories needs to be the Credit Manager once he or she is satisfied that the deal proposed is worth having - if it's lukewarm or distasteful send it straight back.

Tone and evidence

This is where it gets difficult. Commercial landlords are at the mercy of their external valuers whose job is to assess a property and put a sensible value on it. In so doing they will look at the level of rents receivable, the length of the leases, the number of void (empty) units, and increasingly, the financial strength of the tenants. This valuation is incorporated into the published financials of the landlord company, and is a one of the key performance indicators and drivers of investment into the business.

There will therefore be occasions when your friends in the letting and asset management teams will place an appalling proposal under your nose and tell you it is a great one, simply because the level of rent involved is astronomic and will positively affect the valuation of the property the next time it's done.

The fact that the proposed tenant doesn't have anything like the financial wherewithal to withstand a rent of this size, and will become insolvent as soon as the rent free period ends is immaterial, as the rental evidence set by this deal will enable the letting team to justify unsustainably high rents to other new tenants in the property which will also come back and bite them before too long.

Investors love all this of course, as the NAV (net asset value) of the business will undoubtedly increase, but they will be less impressed with the position two years down the road, when half the tenants in a property are insolvent, and the landlord begins to haemorrhage money on business rates as liquidators disclaim the leases.

It's actually far better for the long term survival of the landlord to prioritise the covenant strength or financial status of the tenant over the achievable level of rent, as a property filled with better capitalised tenants will be more stable in terms of rental income, will have fewer insolvencies, will be better advertised, will attract more customers, and will be better able to withstand the slings and arrows of an economic downturn.

There is little the Credit Manager can do to influence this sort of thinking other than by pointing out the pitfalls and making everybody aware of the financial consequences. Sadly little happens until he can say "I told you so" to someone who previously took no notice. But after this inevitable (and rather enjoyable) milestone in the relationship, the Credit Manager is perfectly positioned to maximise his or her influence over the viability of lettings, and once the others involved realise that the dialogue is worthwhile and that it will lead to an easier life, things should get a bit better.

This view will not necessarily be shared by one group of people who will privately (but never publicly) disagree with me. Certain external Letting Agents who survive by brokering lettings with landlords and their tenant clients have little or no interest in the long term survival of independent tenants, because once the deal has been completed and their commission paid, they move on - until that is, the original tenant goes bust, and they can earn another fee by letting the same unit all over again.

This is probably a little unfair on the better agents out there – indeed I was once at an industry function where I bumped into a prominent agent who began to admonish me for a) making his job much more difficult by asking for tenants' financial data, b) stopping him getting (in his opinion) good deals through, and c) generally ruining his life. I asked him "ok then, how many deals which were worth having in the first place have you lost because of me?" After a long pause he finally replied "probably none actually", and I'm not sure which one of us was more shocked by that admission.

It takes time and quite a few "I told you so" scenarios to get to this point of course, but it's very worthwhile when you get there as you've gained the respect of your colleagues and counterparties as a valuable cog in the company wheel, and as I mentioned in the introduction, that's what it's really all about.

Fixed charges

In addition to the standard "Fixed and Floating Charge" which a lender will place over a company's assets in exchange for advancing the money, some lenders place a "Fixed Charge" over a specific lease. Generally speaking the landlord's consent is required, and this is "not to be unreasonably refused" which in reality means you have to have a very good reason to refuse. In practice there are no grounds to refuse unless the tenant is already in breach of the lease terms, or about to go bust, and that's something that should already be evident.

If consent cannot reasonably be refused, the one thing to double check is that the landlord's alienation rights under the lease are not impacted by the letter of consent he is being asked to sign. Alienation rights are stipulations over the type of occupier that can be installed into a property, and effectively give the landlord first refusal when one tenant attempts to assign the lease to another.

The purposes of these rights vary, on the one hand you have morality clauses covering the type of business which can be conducted from the property, but they also cover such things as retail tenant mix (you don't want a chip shop next to an exclusive high end fashion operator) and the financial status of the proposed assignee, as a significant dilution in the covenant of the tenant company is the most common objection. It is therefore imperative that these rights are preserved once the fixed charge is in place, and it's always worth a telephone call to the lawyers just to make sure.

In the event that the tenant breaches the terms of its loan from the charge holder, the charge holder will take control of the lease which it will see as a piece of real estate, and then seek to maximise its value by assigning it to a third party for a financial premium. This is the point when alienation rights are paramount for the reasons already described.

I don't like fixed charges as they complicate the landlord and tenant relationship, with the charge holder having to be party to all future negotiations, but in reality there isn't much the landlord can do about them if his rights under the lease aren't adversely affected.

The Tenant

Tenants are the lifeblood of the landlord's business and it's very easy to forget the fact that they are out to steal from the landlord wherever and whenever possible.

That was a provocative statement designed to raise an eyebrow or two but I made it for a reason.

It's very important to remember that the landlord and tenant relationship is a two way street. For example one rarely sees tenants offering to pay the landlord a bit more rent when things are going well; but when times are hard they cue up to ask for rent concessions, changes to lease terms or outright surrenders, all of which involve the landlord foregoing his contractual income either totally or in part.

A tenancy is by definition a long term relationship and once the documents are signed and exchanged, there's no getting out of it, so we need to find out as much about the other party as possible before the point of no return.

Identity

We've already discussed this in section "The Contract" and I can't stress enough how important it is to get the right counterparty details not only on the landlord's database, but on the tenancy documents themselves. If the Credit Manager has installed himself in the leasing process correctly he should have sight of the engrossed documents before final signoff, and one of the key checks is that the counterpart named in the definitions section of the lease, is the correct one and not a newly incorporated subsidiary company of the main group for example. If the contract has been agreed with such a subsidiary in the first place that's fine, but in that case it follows that all the financial checks must be carried out on the specific tenant company as well as the group as a whole.

Financial status

Can the tenant afford to pay the rent being demanded? Assume it can't until proven otherwise, and let the tenant do the convincing.

Often the only bit of financial information supplied by a prospective tenant (or its highly incentivised agent) is a positive EBITDA figure (Earnings Before Interest, Tax, and Depreciation). This is all very nice, but it only tells us one thing - that the tenant has the real or estimated capacity to earn a certain amount of money FOR ITSELF.

There is no obligation for the tenant to retain any of this money within its corporate structure, or to improve the operating company's financial status at all. In fact if (as is often the case) there is a debt vehicle further up the corporate ladder in the form of a parent company which controls the centralised borrowings for the group, much of this cash will need to be sent up there by way of a management charge to pay off the debt and the interest thereon.

Dividend payments to shareholders are another financial drain. Small companies often pay their principals by way of dividends rather than salaries and there is no way of knowing how much will be taken in a given year. For these reasons I'm never particularly interested in EBITDA, and I tend to look at the balance sheet first, and the profit and loss account second.

The balance sheet tells you how things were at a certain point in time, and the profit and loss (or income statement if you're younger than me) tells you how they got there.

Ultimately we need to see the tangible net worth of the business, as this gives us a devil's advocate position on the actual value of the company on break up, and we can therefore judge for ourselves if the enterprise is of sufficient financial status to honour its commitments (including the payment of rent, service charges, insurance, and other payments due to the landlord).

The big credit agencies (and we'll come onto these) provide financial summaries which include a tangible net worth figure, but if you are relying on standard form accounts filed at Companies House, this figure can be arrived at by subtracting the intangible assets (and investments if shown) from the shareholders' funds figure at the bottom of the balance sheet.

Intangible assets are just that – assets which the company's auditors can't put a value on, and may include such things as intellectual property / trademarks, bespoke software or plant which is worth nothing to anyone else, investments in third parties, and the big one – goodwill.

Goodwill appears when one company acquires another, and represents money paid in excess of the target company's fair market value. The buyer clearly thought it was a good idea to pay this amount of money and wants to reflect the new asset in its books as if it was worth every penny. Auditors tend to take a different view however, and strip out these overpayments as intangibles, so for the purpose of arriving at a failsafe assessment of the proposed tenant's financial status, so should we.

Multipliers

We need to establish a set of minimum key performance indicators which show us that the tenant can withstand the proposed level of rent, and these should include the annual turnover, pre-tax profits, and, as already mentioned, tangible net worth. Rather than having to write lengthy analyses of each proposed tenant's business model as they come along and justify your conclusions in isolation every time, it's a good idea to establish some standard corporate financial tests which all proposed tenants need to pass. If they satisfy these criteria then everybody is happy with the proposed covenant and the deal can move on to the next stage, if they don't then as a Credit Professional it's your job to find a solution which de risks the proposal for the landlord. The ultimate solution of course is not contracting with a high risk tenant in the first place, and that is one of the options available to you if all else fails. I have used the following formulae over many years and applied them successfully to every class of tenant you can think of, as rental commitments tend to rise in proportion with the size of the business:

1. Annual Turnover needs to be ten times the total rental exposure to the tenant.

2. Pre Tax Profits need to be three times the total rental exposure to the tenant.

3. Tangible Net Worth needs to be five times the total rental exposure to the tenant.

All of the above must be demonstrated in filed accounts for three successive years.

These criteria are simple, easy to remember, and can be used by everyone in the landlord's hierarchy without them having to be familiar with accounting. Furthermore, once they are established in the landlord's corporate procedures they provide an easy like for like comparison when comparing one tenant to another, either when deciding which one to go with, or for retrospective analysis of the landlord's portfolio.

By "total rental exposure" I mean the gross annual or passing rent due to the landlord for all the tenant's units in the portfolio, so if tenant A has nine existing units and wants to add another, the calculation needs to include the rental income for all ten.

The clever bit of course is getting the deal over the line when the tenant fails one or more of the tests without taking any risks yourself. I nearly put unnecessary risks there, but there's really no such thing as a necessary risk – a risk is idiomatically a risk, and the outcome is therefore unpredictable.

To base your future income on something which might or might not work strikes me as a bit daft, and even if you end up walking away, you at least have certainty.

This is all fine in an ideal world where tenants are lining up to take units on sellers' terms, but landlords' portfolios vary, and a landlord which owns super prime properties in city centres will be able to dictate terms in a way that a regional owner of secondary properties can only dream of.

However it's still bad practice to take on tenants of questionable financial status unless the worst possible outcome still yields a benefit such as business rates mitigation, or a large central unit in a shopping centre being open and trading over Christmas and boosting footfall for the whole centre as a result.

Security

If the proposed tenant fails one or more of the financial tests, it's not the end of the world as there are several options open to the landlord, none of which will completely protect him from the effect of an insolvent tenant, but which will soften the financial blow significantly.

Rental smoothing

Where a proposed deal includes a rent free period of say 6 months – supposedly to cover fit out and recruitment costs, the terms can be changed to provide for half rent for the full year instead, with payments commencing on the completion date. This way the tenant still pays the same amount of rent for the first year, but it means that the landlord starts receiving income right away. If the worst does happen and the tenant becomes insolvent before the six month point, under the original terms the landlord will have received no rent at all, but if smoothing has been agreed he will at least have received 3 months' worth.

Capital contributions

Handing over money to tenants as part of a letting deal is a fact of life. However we need to be certain that the benefit gained from the landlord's contribution is confined to the unit in question and not a mechanism whereby a tenant can fund the running of its entire business at the landlord's expense. Free money from landlords is much better than an interest bearing loan from a financial institution, so we need to make sure that the contribution is a) justified in the first place, b) that it will be spent on what it's supposed to be spent on, and more significantly, c) that it won't disappear altogether.

There will always be situations where the leasing team will agree to provide a "sweetener" in the form of a capital contribution to get a desirable tenant to sign on the dotted line, and in such cases it won't be possible to see physical evidence of where the money went (such as an extensive store refit or the construction of an escalator for example), but the important issue once again is the creditworthiness of the tenant. Providing no questions asked free funding to an undercapitalised tenant about to collapse into insolvency isn't particularly clever, and once again a full evaluation of the potential tenant's financial status, utilising the standard financial criteria discussed in the section "Multipliers" will give an early indication of financial risk and prevent the landlord from unnecessary loss.

Where there is some uncertainty over the tenant's solvency and the contribution is designed to improve the fabric (and therefore the capital value in the landlord's books) of the unit in question, paying the builders or shop fitters directly and sidestepping the tenant completely is one remedy, or alternatively paying the tenant only once the works have been completed and on production of invoices from the builders or shop fitters is another. Ideally the landlord would like to see the works completed and the unit opened for trade before the money is paid over, as this not only safeguards the investment, but an objection can indicate that the tenant has inadequate financial headroom for the project in the first place. Knowing about a problem is the first step in avoiding it, and once that capital payment has been made it's never coming back.

Rent deposits

Landlords like rent deposits but tenants don't. This blindingly obvious and rather fatuous statement isn't simply referring to the dead money tied up in a deposit account which the tenant would rather have access to, but to something more far reaching:-

Apart from the requirement that all rent deposits which accrue interest must be held in an independent bank account; since the Enterprise Act 2003 all deposits need to be subject to a registered charge if they are to be of any value. The Deed of Charge (Rent Deposit Deed) must be registered at Companies House, as without this a clever insolvency practitioner can claim the deposit is money merely held by the landlord on trust for the tenant, and demand its return – thereby defeating the object completely.

The important thing about Rent Deposit Deeds is that they are public notice documents, and therefore not only visible to anyone with a Companies House subscription, but to all the credit rating agencies and their customers as well. Tenants will sometimes try and avoid giving a rent deposit, purely because as soon as one is registered everybody else can see it and the precedent is clearly established.

Remarkably some tenants are unaware of this and commence leasing negotiations with the statement that they do not, never have, and never will give a rent deposit, only to be presented with a Dun & Bradstreet or Experian report showing numerous deposits given to other landlords throughout the years. I don't generally enjoy humiliating people, but I'll happily bend the rules a bit when I'm being deliberately lied to.

Parental guarantees

We've already touched on the subject of tenants applying for leases in the name of low value subsidiary companies of a larger group, and in such circumstances the remedies involve tracking up the tenant's corporate tree until you find a group company which fulfils the landlord's standard financial criteria, and either insisting that a) the lease is taken in the name of this superior company (not always possible) or b) that the parent provides a guarantee over all the obligations and liabilities of the subsidiary under the lease, including the payment of rents and other charges due. The relationship between the guarantor and the principal tenant will not feature in credit reports unless there is a separate Deed of Guarantee filed at Companies House, because in most cases the guarantor and its obligations will simply be added to the main lease. As a result a parental guarantee is often far more palatable for the tenant not only because it doesn't tie up cash, but also because it will not be widely publicised. There are two areas where this can fall down however:

1. Where the proposed guarantor is the top company in a large group such as a FTSE 100 Plc, and where a Board Meeting would be required to approve the guarantee terms. For obvious reasons one cannot expect this to happen every time a subsidiary company wants to open a new shop, so another form of security needs to be found.

2. Where the guarantor has restrictions on contingent liabilities dictated by its lenders. Even though a parental guarantee is not publicly filed information and will not show up on a commercial credit report, it does need to be reflected in the notes to the guarantor's accounts (usually at about note 20). A bank or venture capital company may not be too keen on the recipient of its finances entering into guarantee arrangements with (possibly speculative) subsidiaries, and will prohibit this kind of activity completely. Once again another form of security needs to be found.

Incidentally it's always a good idea to look at the last couple of notes appended to any company's annual accounts, as they will often contain highly significant information such as post balance sheet events including new funding, share issues, and changes of control, related party transactions including inter group loans, and the aforementioned contingent liabilities and guarantees.

Personal guarantees

Personal guarantees are both a blessing and a curse depending on what you are trying to achieve.

On the one hand a personal guarantor is effectively signing over the realisation of all his assets in order to pay the charges due under the lease, regardless of whether the property continues to generate income or not. There is no limited liability company to hide behind, and unless the individual has significant personal wealth (in which case he'll be unlikely to risk it anyway), the end result is likely to be either a Bankruptcy Order or an IVA (Individual Voluntary Arrangement – more on these later).

On the other hand the proposed guarantor may be a man of straw with little in the way of assets to draw upon. If the guarantor cannot pay the rent on behalf of the defaulting tenant, and the landlord has exhausted all recovery options, then a bankruptcy petition filed by the landlord will only serve to invite all the guarantor's creditors to submit claims. This will inevitably include the dreaded HMRC who have a habit of barging in and taking the lion's share of whatever is available, leaving the landlord and other creditors high and dry.

Does all this mean that personal guarantees are therefore worthless? No it doesn't - far from it in fact.

The personal guarantee's value lies in its power as a deterrent; nobody wants to lose everything they have to pay off the debts of a defunct business, so being personally on the hook for the rent means that the guarantor will ensure that the tenant complies with its responsibilities to the best of his ability. Also in a scenario where a tenant has a number of trading units priority will be given to those with guarantees, so rather than the guarantee just being a means of recovering money, it's far more effective as a way of ensuring compliance.

Moreover, if the worst should happen and the trading company is placed in administration or a CVA (Company Voluntary Arrangement – more on these later as well), the guaranteed units will almost certainly continue to trade with full rent being paid, as the guarantor will be personally liable for any shortfall. So once again the presence of the guarantee helps to ensure that the landlord's forecasted income is preserved throughout the bad times, as well as giving the landlord an avenue for debt recovery as a last resort.

Other landlords

Having completed the financial evaluation of a tenant, and asked for a deposit or guarantee as it fails one or more of the standard financial criteria, the response most often received from the other side is "no other landlord has asked us for this". Now the tenant (or its agent – highly incentivised remember) clearly thinks that this revelation will force the landlord to see the error of his ways and commit financial suicide by relying on his word about the opinions of others.

My reply is always "more fool them then!" as I have more confidence in my own ability to evaluate a prospective tenant's creditworthiness than anyone else's. What the tenant actually means (if it's at all true of course) is that the other landlords haven't done their homework and are taking unnecessary risks. This could either be because they were desperate to install the tenant in an empty unit where there were no alternatives, that the rent offered was so attractive in raising the overall valuation of the centre that they snapped the tenant's hand off, or just that they don't have adequate procedures in place to identify risky tenants, relying on a hit and hope strategy aka pure luck. Too many people give too little thought to what might happen if the deal they've just signed doesn't turn out the way that they expected, and where a property company is chiefly inhabited and controlled by Surveyors, risk management is too often at the bottom of the totem pole in terms of priority.

Given that the landlord community is quite incestuous due to personnel moving from one company to another, and that most sensible Credit Professionals will gladly forge reciprocal relationships with their competitors' opposite numbers, the quick fix here is to ask the other landlords if the tenant is telling the truth, and whether any security was obtained to cover the poor covenant.

This all seems rather obvious but you'd be surprised at the number of people who don't double check what the other side are telling them, even though their claim will provide them with a clear advantage.

This sharing of information between landlords has other benefits as well, as it prevents situations where a tenant will only approach a less financially astute landlord because the clever one down the road will ask for a deposit or guarantee. So if landlord A successfully completes a letting which involves a deposit or a guarantee, he should have no reservations about letting landlords B to Z know about it, as it levels the playing field and focuses competition between property companies on the areas that letting teams are good at (rental levels, unit size and suitability etc.), and does away with situations where a tenant will take an unsuitable unit purely because its financials will not be properly scrutinised.

Types of Tenant

This brings us on to which of the procedures outlined above are appropriate for the different types of tenant likely to come across your desk.

Sole proprietorships

A single person trading as anything other than a limited company is a sole proprietor, and can be a mixed blessing for the landlord. In the section on personal guarantees I covered the pros and cons of limited liability, and as the sole proprietor or sole trader is effectively standing as a personal guarantor for himself, the same advantages and disadvantages apply. The financial strength of the individual is the total worth of all his personal assets less all liabilities. This means the value of all the equipment used for the running of the business, the car or van, the individual's personal or family residence (if he owns one), right down to bank balances, clothes, and whatever he keeps in the shed, less outstanding mortgages on property, unpaid tax (usually the big one), business loans (more than likely to be secured on property), along with personal finance debts, and any other amounts due to be paid for whatever reason.

Now as there is no requirement for an individual to have his accounts audited, it can be virtually impossible to accurately assess his financial standing - indeed most of us would struggle to assess our own in any amount of detail. A solicitor can (for a fee) perform an asset check involving a Land Registry search, which will flag up whether the individual owns any property (and any unpaid mortgages or charges registered against it), and a consumer credit report from Call Credit or Experian will reveal any existing or previous judgements as well as confirmation that the person is who he says he is, and that he lives where he says he does.

I must stress the importance of obtaining a residential address for any sole proprietor – the trading unit address is not sufficient - as it will be impossible to serve legal documents on the individual once he has cleared the premises of stock and equipment and absconded without paying his rent.

Most credit agencies will ask you for two recent utility bills with your name and address on before they will give you credit, and you should do the same with a proposed tenant if corporate financial information is unavailable.

Notwithstanding all this, the existence of personal liability for all the debts of his business will automatically focus the sole trader's mind on avoiding upsetting his creditors at all costs. Even if all the proprietor's personal possessions miraculously turn out to be owned by someone else ("ah but that's the wife's car you see") the ultimate sanction is still his personal bankruptcy, and regardless of what anybody says in these enlightened times, there is still a stigma attached to that, and not to mention a lot of inconvenience for the person concerned and his nearest and dearest.

Regardless of whether you consider the prudence imposed on the prospective tenant by personal liability to outweigh the possibility that he may be a man of straw, the only real way to be certain that you are not taking a risk is to request a rent deposit, and if the tenant can't stump up a minimum of three months' rent, then his business is insufficiently capitalised.

Once a deposit has been refused then all things being equal you shouldn't be considering this sole trader as a tenant, as his business plan will be based on optimism and good intentions rather than sensible projections, and if it all goes wrong for him it will go wrong for you as well.

Sureties

A surety is a traditional term for a third party personal guarantor, so the financial evaluation of the principal tenant needs to be extended to cover the surety as well. Everything I've already said about the sole trader applies equally to the surety, with the additional benefit that the surety will be keeping a very close eye on how the proprietor is running his business in order to avoid having to pay out money himself. Furthermore in my experience the surety is more likely to face up to a problem before it becomes critical and engage with the landlord than the proprietor, who will often be in denial until it's too late.

Partnerships

A partnership is a number of individuals whose business is conducted under a common trading style, and can also be referred to as a "firm". More often than not a partnership will relate to a small or medium service enterprise where the only commodity being marketed is expertise, such as a consultancy or firm of lawyers. The "partners" can then be paid directly out of the firm's takings, accounting for their own income tax liabilities as if they were self-employed.

In such cases the partners should be treated as multiple sole proprietors who are jointly and severally liable for the partnership's debts – indeed all invoices should be raised against the individuals "trading as" in order for the debt to be easily recoverable via the courts. Otherwise much time can be wasted establishing that the individuals are personally liable, with the burden of proof resting on the landlord.

There are of course some large partnerships out there which have integrated management structures with jointly held "partnership assets" which produce audited accounts, thereby making the job of financial evaluation much easier for the landlord . However the unlimited liability of the individual partners for the firm's debts makes this an undesirable legal basis for any sizeable business. Where there are large financial obligations but no physical sales you are far more likely to find that the other side have sought to protect themselves by forming a limited liability partnership.

Limited liability partnerships (LLPs)

The worst of all worlds – the partners are protected by limited liability but the financial transparency provided by a limited company's requirement to submit annual audited accounts is entirely absent. For this reason one must be careful when entering into leases with LLPs, as they are often a complete unknown from a covenant point of view. The credit rating agencies aren't much help either, as there will be no financial or Gazette information to accurately base their recommendations on. One such agency used to give all LLPs a £5,000.00 credit limit as a matter of course, and whenever I saw this I'd regard it as their way of saying "We don't know – best of luck!" Not ideal.

In some cases the larger LLPs will take the trouble to submit audited figures on request, but remember this is entirely at their discretion, and just because they published a good set of numbers last year, it doesn't mean that they won't suppress a bad set this year and save themselves an audit fee, so in the absence of a proper audit trail on which to base a financial evaluation, the partners should agree to guarantee the LLP's obligations under the lease, or alternatively to provide the landlord with the universal remedy of a rent deposit.

Incorporation into a limited company

These come up from time to time and can be either a symptom of a successful business, or the precursor of failure. Sooner or later a successful proprietorship will consider incorporating itself into a limited company for a number of reasons.

The first of these is likely to be as a way of limiting the tax liability of the business and retain money in the corporate purse. Above a certain level of turnover it's far more efficient to pay corporation tax on the company's profits than it is to trade as an individual, where the tax man will usually regard the assets of the business as the proprietor's personal possessions until it can be proven otherwise. By forming a limited company the proprietor / director can thereby separate his personal finances from those of the company, receiving shares in exchange for any assets which he is leaving with (or selling to) the company, and as we will see this is both good and bad from a landlord's perspective.

Another reason for incorporation is the formalised organisational structure that limited company status provides, with the regular accounting periods and audited financial disclosure that suppliers, customers, landlords, and lenders seek to rely on. Limited liability is therefore a building block to upsizing a business, particularly when further investment in infrastructure is required, providing transparency, accepted standards of disclosure, and straightforward benchmarking against other companies in the sector. We all like to see our tenants doing well and incorporation can be an indicator.

The downside of incorporation is that where the landlord was originally dealing with a sole proprietor or partnership where the individuals were personally liable for the debts of the business, unless he is careful he will now be dealing with a corporate institution with limited means, and where the directors have managed to ring fence their personal possessions and absolve themselves of personal liability for the rental payments under the lease(s), if the company should go down.

It's not often as simple as that of course, as in many cases directors stand to lose a considerable amount if their business fails, but from the landlord's position any proposed assignment from a proprietorship to a limited company controlled by the same individuals should be firmly resisted, and consent refused on covenant grounds unless:

1. The directors agree to remain as personal guarantors of the company's obligations under the lease for the full period of the term, meaning that the landlord's security is in no way diminished.

2. Where significant investment into the new company or other factors clearly show that the new company's covenant strength is greater than the original proprietor's.

I mentioned that incorporation can be a precursor to a critical situation, and even though it's the exception rather than the rule, it does happen. If you were are sole trader whose business was in financial difficulty, and your personal possessions were likely to be either seized by court or landlord appointed enforcement officers, or sold off by the Trustee in your inevitable bankruptcy. What better way of saving everything you have worked for than by moving the bare bones of your business into a limited liability company, where the amount you are likely to lose is capped and your house and family possessions are protected? This is another reason not to consent to an assignment from an individual or partnership to a limited company under the same control, because you never know what's round the corner and you don't want to be robbed of your security just before the tenant's business falls over.

One final point here is that where such an assignment application has been made, rental payments need to be carefully scrutinised to ensure that they are only accepted from the correct and original tenant, and not the new limited company. This should be a standard check on daily receipts, but it's even more important when a tenant is seeking to change its identity - you don't want to be tricked into regularising a tenancy with a worthless company without any financial security, by an unscrupulous or desperate tenant simply trying to limit his losses by any means available. A commercial landlord is after all not a charity.

Charities

Which neatly brings me onto charities!

Following on from my last comment about landlords it's also rather naive to suggest that a charity is not a business, as the numbers are clearly important if the charity itself is to survive. However I do think landlords generally accept charities for what they are and don't try to charge excessive rents for the best of reasons. The effect of this is that the leases charities take tend to be short, a) so as not to negatively affect the commercial valuation of the landlord's property, and b) to provide the landlord with the flexibility to re let the unit to another tenant at a competitive rent if a better offer comes along.

Indeed many landlords use charities as a method of filling void units and avoiding business rates liabilities by granting short leases on service charge and rates only terms. This situation works for both parties, as the charity are getting a cheap deal, and the landlord is avoiding a local authority rates bill.

However, this isn't always the case, as charities need head offices as well as other institutions, and these will often be on commercial terms, so standard procedures need to be followed as much as possible.

I'm sure I'm not alone in wondering what percentage of any donation I make actually reaches the good cause I am seeking to help, and how much is skimmed off to fund the charity's infrastructure, or to pay those irritating people in the street who don't seem to understand what "no thank you" means.

From a professional point of view however, a landlord should hope that the charity retains as much money and / or assets as possible in order to satisfy the covenant tests which we have discussed at length in previous sections.

By their very nature charities are not profit-making organisations per se, but it's still important to conduct a standard financial assessment in order to ensure that the organisation can comply with the terms contained in the lease. Sometimes this can be problematic, as the quality and timeliness of financial disclosure can vary quite markedly from one charity to another. The Register of Charities website is the obvious place to start, and contains most of the information you will need. Given that charities as a rule do not produce accounts in the same form as a trading company (as the more they spend on auditors and accountants the less goes to the beneficiaries), the available financial information is more often than not confined to annual income and expenditure figures. Charity income of course is not the same as the turnover of a limited company, as (tax allowances notwithstanding) they rely on the generosity of individuals and businesses to simply give them money when it's convenient or fashionable. Marketing does take place of course, and some charities are very good at it, but there is still possibility that one good cause will either fall out of favour or be side-lined by another more high profile or topical fundraising initiative. There is only so much discretionary money around, and charities compete for it, so at the end of the day a lot of their survival does depend on luck.

For this reason it's impossible to predict the future income of a charity with any degree of accuracy regardless of what they tell you, so we are left with no alternative but to subtract the most recent outgoings from the income from the same period, and regard the resulting figure as net worth. I should stress that some charities provide excellent information including detailed overheads, but in many cases this ball park calculation may be all you have to go on. Clearly if the letting is a sizeable on with a significant rent attached to it then it's up to the landlord to ask the charity for enough bespoke financial information to allay any fears, but this is unlikely to be forthcoming for a small unit in a shopping centre or high street.

Government departments

Now this is where it gets really frustrating!

Under this heading I include The Secretary of State, local authorities, NHS Departments, Police and Crime Agencies, The Security Services, and anybody else funded out of the public purse.

The one thing they all have in common is a complete inability to process invoices correctly and / or pay their bills on time. In my younger years when I was collecting commercial debts for supply companies I developed a rule of thumb borne out of bitter experience, that it takes on average 6 telephone calls to a government department to get an invoice paid. If you manage to do it with three calls on one occasion, then the next time it will take you nine.

This state of affairs isn't caused by budget constraints or devious cash management strategies, but more to do with structure, hierarchy and bureaucracy. The problem with all the agencies outlined above is that their accounting sections are part of an enormous interdependent sprawl of public sector departments which have never had to act in a competitive manner, or operate within the timetables that private sector organisations take for granted. I don't mean to undervalue the work the employees of these institutions do (my wife has worked in the library service for over 30 years so I daren't), but in the public sector everything is dominated and subordinated by procedure, including timeliness, efficiency, reason and common sense.

One could argue that having a government funded tenant removes the risk of not getting paid due to insolvency, and this is probably true, however any benefit to be gained in this way is more than offset by the interminable struggle to collect the money that is rightfully yours on the date it is due.

The remedy to all this is to ensure that every possible area for misinterpretation or dispute has been removed from the engrossed tenancy documents as well as the rent, service charge, and insurance demands. If the department you are dealing with requires a purchase order before they can process a rental payment on an existing lease, then sort it out in advance of the due date. If there is an opportunity for the leasing team to cap service charges and fix the quarterly or monthly rate when the deal is done, then I recommend they do it, as it will save a lot of management time later on. The public sector is ingenious when it comes to finding ways of not spending tax payers money on things it has contracted to spend it on, and the fewer open goals you leave them the better – ideally there should be none at all.

Disputes will nevertheless occur, and are often compounded by staff changes within the department you are dealing with. These inevitably lead to regular breakdowns in communication, and infuriating situations where you find yourself dealing with a new contact every few months who probably has no prior knowledge of the issue. It is therefore imperative that you keep an accurate record of all communications to and from the other side. At least this way you won't have to start all over again when the person you have been dealing disappears after a few months, to be replaced (or not) by a probably well-meaning individual who hasn't got a clue what you're talking about. You can often predict when these staff changes will occur, as they tend to coincide with that nice feeling you get when you think you're finally getting somewhere!

All I can do apart from giving the above advice is wish you the very best of luck with this lot.

Private limited companies

The most common form of tenant entity taking space in commercial property is the private limited company. As I covered most of the advantages and disadvantages of limited companies under the section on incorporations, and the qualifying financial criteria in the section entitled multipliers, I don't propose to go through it all again. However there are a few additional points you might want to bear in mind:

1. Anybody can form a limited company, even complete idiots with no experience or ability can buy an off the shelf company and start trading. This way they can ring fence their financial liability to the amount they have personally invested in the company, while at the same time keeping their personal possessions and bank balances out of reach of potential creditors. You should therefore be very suspicious of any company without a trading history, and ask for additional security in the form of a rent deposit or guarantee as a matter of course.

2. Just because the company you are being asked to contract with is part of a large and credit worthy group, do not assume that the group will accept responsibility for the obligations of your counterparty if things start to go

badly. One of the reasons companies set up subsidiaries is to limit the risk of failure of a new venture to that company only, with no contingent financial liability on the other companies in the group. If the subsidiary company should become insolvent and you as landlord have no legal recourse to other group companies, you will be powerless to do anything, and the sight of the unaffected group companies continuing on as if nothing has happened will not be a pleasant one. It is therefore imperative that the financial assessment of any potential tenant is only carried out on the entities you can actually bring proceedings against, whether it is an individual company, or a parent company providing a guarantee. If there is no available counterparty with sufficient financial status to satisfy the standard multipliers we discussed earlier on, then get some other security such as a rent deposit, or a better parental or bank guarantee which can be reliably drawn down on in times of trouble.

3. Company year ends vary, and there is no requirement to file financial results at Companies House before the 9 month deadline. Many companies do of course, but it's important to ensure that the financial data you are reviewing is as current as possible. One regular trick which wily Property Agents will try and fox you with is to voluntarily provide accounts for their clients which tick all the boxes in terms of multipliers and KPIs. However on closer inspection these accounts prove not to be the most recent, but have been superseded by another set which show a significantly poorer picture. It's therefore in your interest to conduct your own enquiries regardless of the information provided by the other side. Credit agencies and Companies House provide impartial and independently audited information, and that's part of what they charge us for. It's also wise to remember that property agents have an agenda of their own - it's called

commission, and the more deals they get over the line, the more they get.

4. Finally it's a good idea to have a more than cursory look at the principals behind any company you might end up contracting with. Has there been a significant change in the management team recently? Has the finance director just resigned (usually a sign of trouble ahead), and most importantly, do you recognise any of the names?

Familiarity with the individuals behind a new venture can breed comfort as well as contempt, but here we're only interested in identifying directors who are either bad businessmen or just downright dishonest. It doesn't take long to mentally compile a list of miscreants once you've been bitten a couple of times, and success at seeing off creditors gives bad directors a false sense of confidence and in some cases a quite brazen attitude. As credit professionals we have a duty to our community to promote best practice, and there's nothing wrong with expecting the same sort of behaviour from others. So when the villains come round again (as they surely will), you will be forewarned and able to avoid dealing with them, or if that's not possible tie them up so tightly with deposits and or guarantee structures, so that when the inevitable happens you will not be unnecessarily damaged.

Public limited companies

It's an old joke that if a company adds "International Ltd" to its title, it's probably nothing of the sort, so a public limited company (Plc) isn't necessarily a respected and well-heeled organisation whose shares are traded every day on the Stock Exchange either. There are entry requirements such as a minimum share capital (at the time of writing) of £50k, but that does not mean that the company is worth that much or is even in the black at all. Large public companies issue interim management statements at their half year point which provide a "work in progress" view of how they are dong compared to their forecasts, and this will almost certainly provoke some negative press comment if things aren't going well. This freely available information flow cuts both ways, as it helps you to monitor your tenant more efficiently, but it also allows other stakeholders to react as well, and they can do it far more quickly than the landlord can. This means that faced with negative comments about business X in the media, the trade suppliers will withhold further supply in order to limit their exposure, possibly causing a cash flow problem for the tenant and compounding its misery. More importantly if credit insurance companies are involved, they may well pull the suppliers' cover, signalling a further lack of confidence and ultimately the beginning of the end for the tenant.

There isn't much the landlord can do in these situations other than watch helplessly as the events unfold, so proper financial evaluation of the tenant remains paramount. Granted a lot can change over a lease term of 10 years, and the highly regarded household name can mutate into an outdated and underappreciated dinosaur (and yes I'm thinking of poor old Woolworths), but you have a much better chance of avoiding these situations by focusing on the numbers, rather than by just hoping for the best.

Subtenants

You might argue "why should a landlord be bothered about the creditworthiness of a subtenant?" After all the principal tenant retains all the lease liabilities including the obligation to pay the landlord all the money due under the lease, regardless of whether he manages to collect it from the subtenant or not. So if we do a proper credit check on the principal tenant we're protected aren't we?

Not necessarily – I always look at subtenants as if they are principals because of the following possibilities:

1. The principal tenant becomes insolvent. If the subtenant is trading well he may wish to take over the principal lease, you will therefore need to run the standard checks at this point anyway. Moreover, if it's becoming clear that the principal tenant is on a downward spiral, knowing the financial status of the subtenant (as well as the unit cost to turnover ratio) will help you manage the risk across your portfolio. You will then be able to take proactive steps to regularise the tenancy of the subtenant and avoid a void.

2. The subtenant becomes insolvent. Just because you have a robust tenant evaluation procedure in place, don't assume that your tenant has carried out the same amount of due diligence when subletting to someone else. It's important therefore, to know what calibre of operator is occupying your unit and how financially sound it is. The principal tenant may only find out that something is seriously wrong when the subtenant's rent doesn't arrive when it should, and a letter from an insolvency practitioner drops through the letterbox instead. If the principal tenant is relying on the subtenant's rent in order to pay the superior rent to the landlord, debt recovery action may result in an insolvent principal tenant as well. Monitoring the subtenant as if they were a principal won't stop this happening of course, but it will enable you to adjust your leasing strategy and line up a replacement tenant well in advance if you have prior knowledge of a critical situation.

3. There is a dispute between the tenant and subtenant, and no rent is paid by the subtenant to the tenant. If the tenant does not pay the rent to the landlord he is at risk

of debt recovery action, but in some cases the tenant will be relying on the subtenant's money, so debt recovery could actually lead to the tenant becoming insolvent. This helps nobody, so a better way of resolving the matter is to threaten to regularise the subtenant either by forfeiting the principal tenancy (using non-payment of rent as the breach), or by issuing a Section 81 Notice under the Landlords, Courts and Tribunals Act (more on this later). Either way you will end up with a direct relationship with the former subtenant, and knowing as much as you can about them in advance will help you decide whether they are worth engaging with at all, and if so on the most effective strategy.

4. The subtenant absconds leaving the principal tenant with a rent bill for a unit he is not using, and may now not be able to afford. Once again debt recovery litigation is available to the landlord, but it may make the situation even worse. Far better to monitor the subtenant as if they were a "proper" tenant, thereby giving the landlord as much of an early warning of the subtenant's behaviour as possible. This way the tenant and landlord might be able to work together to head off a problem by perhaps agreeing a rent concession (which must of course filter through to the subtenant!) in exchange for a landlord break, or perhaps by agreeing to market the unit to find a replacement subtenant.

Assignments

Unless specifically agreed in writing otherwise, an assignment simply means that another party takes over what's left of the lease, including all the tenant's obligations, until the original expiry date. It is therefore important to subject the assignee to the same due diligence which was applied to the assignor, as the landlord and tenant relationship will be the same, with only the tenant's name on the lease changing.

A formal application to assign a lease to another party will typically allow the landlord 28 days to give consent (not to be unreasonably refused), or provide a good reason to reject the application. Aside from tenant mix and usage issues, the main reason for objection is usually covenant dilution, or in other words the proposed assignee is of a poorer financial standing than the assignor, thereby increasing the perceived credit risk to the landlord. Where the reduction in creditworthiness is self-evident – a FTSE 100 company assigning to a start-up for example – it's unlikely that the landlord's objection will be challenged in court, but where the difference is marginal it can be more difficult, and this is where a proper analysis of the assignee's financials will be essential if for some reason the landlord doesn't want to go along with the proposal.

AGAs, GAGAs, and Good Harvest

Although they sound like baby talk, the first two of these are mnemonics for valuable remedies to covenant dilution on assignments, and the third is a pivotal piece of case law which governs their use.

An AGA, or Authorised Guarantee Agreement, is a guarantee by the outgoing assignor of the incoming assignee's obligations under the lease until the expiry date. This effectively means that the landlord retains the benefit of the original tenant's covenant, and can call on it to fulfil the lease obligations if the assignee fails to do so for whatever reason including insolvency. Under the AGA, if the assignor is required to step in and fulfil the tenant's lease obligations, it will be able to legally reclaim the right to a principal tenancy, or in other words to get the assigned lease back. The value of the AGA is therefore dependant on the financial stability of the assignor, so if the original tenant's covenant is on the slide, its existence could over time become worthless. However in such cases the landlord will usually be keen to approve an assignment from a bad company to a good one without the requirement for an AGA from the bad one.

AGAS are not automatic, and must be based on a reasonable request, meaning that the landlord will have to justify the need in court if challenged. They are well worth holding out for however, as the refusal by an assignor to give one can be based on strategic moves which the landlord should investigate, and which could provide pointers to the assignor's future behaviour elsewhere in the landlord's portfolio. If the assignor refuses to give an AGA in order to get it off the hook with this particular lease, then the landlord should ask why. Could the assignor be pulling out of the market? Could it have no faith in longevity of the assignee? Could it know something about the unit itself which has escaped everybody else's attention? I always err on the side of suspicion, as even if it's unfounded you're no worse off, and everybody can see that you're doing your job properly.

Where the assignor has the benefit of a parental or personal guarantee relating to its own obligations under the lease, this guarantee will usually (unless specifically stripped out in the assignment documents) cover the assignor's obligations under an AGA. This is a GAGA, or a Guaranteed Authorised Guarantee Agreement. Where it all gets complicated is where an assignor's guarantor seeks to directly guarantee the obligations of the assignee, as this is illegal due to a piece of case law called Good Harvest Partnership LLP v Centaur Services Ltd, commonly known as Good Harvest. This legal authority only allows an assignor's guarantor to underwrite the obligations of the assignee by way of guaranteeing the assignor's obligations under an AGA.

Simply put, an assignor's guarantor cannot also act as a direct guarantor of an assignee, but it can guarantee the assignor's obligations under an AGA, so if there is no AGA in place there can be no guarantee from the assignor's side of the deal.

Other remedies can also apply to covenant dilution on assignments, such as a rent deposit from the assignee, or the assignee's own parental guarantee. These are sometimes the preferred option if there are doubts about the assignor's long term survival, as they take the assignor completely out of the picture.

Assignments between group companies

Some leases contain specified Group Sharing Provisions, and these usually apply to large companies with numerous brand names, each having its own trading entity, but all of which are consolidated under one ultimate holding company. Group Sharing Provisions are designed to provide the tenant with flexibility over which brand name is operating from a particular property, with the name of the tenant on the lease remaining the same regardless of the subsidiary company actually trading from the unit.

Where no such Group Sharing Provision exists, an assignment between members of the same organisation should be treated just like any other assignment, as the covenant of the assignee will be the one the landlord is interested in. As already mentioned the fact that a tenant is a subsidiary of a large successful group does not mean that the group will ensure that the tenant continues to trade and pay its bills when times get tough, so an assignee in an inter group assignment needs to be treated as if it is a standalone company, and its financials reviewed accordingly.

AGAs and GAGAs still apply and can be very useful in these situations but you need to be very careful that intercompany assignments do not contravene Good Harvest, particularly in cases where one group company typically guarantees the obligations of all the trading subsidiaries.

In these situations subletting by one group company to another may be a solution, as the principal tenant remains unchanged, however the proposed subtenant should still be subject to a standard credit check for all the reasons mentioned in the section "AGAS, GAGAs & Good Harvest".

Privity of Contract and Section 17 notices

We're seeing fewer and fewer of these as time goes on, but for a lease with a commencement date prior to 1st January 1996, Privity of Contract applies, giving landlords an additional angle if an assignee breaches the lease terms or becomes insolvent.

Privity of Contract was abolished by the Landlord & Tenant Covenants Act 1995, which came into effect on 1st January 1996. For leases dated 1995 and before, this effectively means that the original counterparties referred to on the lease documents can never fully absolve themselves of responsibility for the covenants / obligations under the lease. When a Surveyor refers to an "old lease" he usually means one of these.

In a scenario where an assignee has fallen into administration, and is neither trading from the unit under the control of the administrators nor paying the rent, the landlord can wind the clock back to the previous leaseholder by way of a Section 17 Notice, and call on that party to comply with the lease provisions. The quid pro quo for this compliance is the right for the previous incumbent to take an overriding lease, or in other words get the tenancy back, and this is clearly fair and equitable.

Where a lease has been assigned more than once, the landlord can issue repeated Section 17 Notices against the previous leaseholders in order, until one of them remedies whatever breach has occurred and takes on the responsibility for the lease from that point onwards. If there is no willing historical tenant willing to take this on, the landlord can litigate, as the obligations of previous tenants bound under Privity are legally enforceable.

A word of caution though, as the landlord should examine the financial strength of the previous tenant and decide whether he wants to re-enter that relationship, because as already mentioned, he cannot cherry pick which part of the tenancy he wishes to transfer – it's all or nothing. It may of course be that the previous tenant is now insolvent as well, so Privity is no help at all. But even if that's not the case the landlord will still be opening himself up to the risk that the previous leaseholder, now saddled with the lease on a property it thought it had got rid of, will immediately attempt to assign it again to a new third party, and may not be too choosy about who it is. Given that the onus is on the landlord to justify a refusal to give consent to an assignment, Section 17 actions should always be thought through very carefully.

A further point worth remembering is that where lawyers get involved, fees follow, and contentious situations where no party wants to accept liability can be unpredictable in both their outcome and the associated legal expense. So if a Section 17 Notice under Privity is an option, do make sure it's the best one before pressing the go button.

Payment Terms

Monthly, quarterly, or only when you catch them

Quarterly rents payable in advance have been fairly standard across the commercial property industry since the nineteenth century, prior to which rents were usually paid in arrears. However since the credit crunch in the late noughties more and more commercial tenants are requesting and securing monthly rental payments.

There is no shortage of reasons why monthly rental payments benefit the tenant community, and in situations where cash flow is tight it can mean the difference between the landlord having a living tenant and a void. However the idea that the frequency of rental payments is of little interest to landlords is simply not true for reasons we'll come onto in a moment, but to analyse the situation correctly it's probably helpful to set out the advantages and disadvantages that the different types of rental payment give each counterparty under the lease:-

Quarterly in advance

Landlord positives - improved cash flow, guaranteed income for three months from the due date, efficient forecasting, increased bank interest, cheaper credit insurance, more cash available to invest in further development, three months protection against the insolvency of the tenant, fewer opportunities for the tenant to delay rental payments in favour of payments to other creditors, and lower administration fees as rents only need to be collected four times a year.

Landlord negatives - lack of flexibility as the tenancy is assured for three months from the due date and the ability to forfeit for strategic reasons is therefore not available, and restricted leasing opportunities as fewer tenants are now willing to sign up to quarterly rental payments.

Tenant positives – lower administration burden as rents only have to be paid four times a year, improved security as the landlord's ability to employ strategic forfeiture is removed for three months from the due date, and ironically more comfort to the tenant's investors who will know that a key overhead has been discharged for three months.

Tenant negatives – the requirement to tie up operating capital which could be used elsewhere in the short term, quarterly spikes in outgoing rental payments often requiring a bank overdraft facility to accommodate them, and fewer opportunities to withhold rent in the event of a dispute with the landlord.

Monthly in advance

Landlord positives – earlier warning of tenant insolvency, increased opportunity for strategic forfeiture, and can preserve a tenancy of a struggling tenant where cash flow is the problem.

Landlord negatives – reduced protection against tenant insolvency, higher level of scrutiny required of tenant performance, more expensive credit insurance, income only guaranteed for one month from the payment date, reduced bank interest receivable, increased administration costs due to more frequent billing and reporting, and increased opportunities for the tenant to withhold payment for whatever reason.

Tenant positives – improved cash flow management, regularised outgoings without quarterly peaks requiring costly overdraft facilities, more opportunities to withhold rent in the event of a dispute with the landlord, and more opportunities to delay payment to the landlord and give other creditors priority.

Tenant negatives - increased time spent on administration due to more frequent billing, increased risk of strategic forfeiture by the landlord, increased scrutiny of performance by the landlord, other lease terms impacted by increased number of payment dates.

Commuting quarterly leases to monthly

Many leases are already negotiated on the basis of monthly rents from the outset, and this is clearly the way the wind is blowing for the industry, in fact it doesn't require a great feat of imagination to predict that in not too many years' time a quarterly lease will be shown as an onerous lease provision in a typical company's annual audited accounts. The movement to monthly rents across the industry is therefore gradual and manageable as old quarterly leases expire and new monthly leases replace them.

The issue for landlords is where a lease was entered into on quarterly terms in good faith, and where the tenant now wants to vary the terms to monthly, with all other lease provisions remaining unchanged. The lease will have been agreed by both sides with their eyes wide open, and payment terms will without doubt have impacted other areas of the agreement - for example the rent free period may have been reduced or a capital payment increased by the leasing team, in the knowledge that the risk of the tenant becoming insolvent will have been mitigated to some extend by the landlord being paid three months in advance at a time. It is therefore inappropriate for a tenant to assume that it can vary one lease term in isolation without revisiting the entire deal.

Most landlords have experienced the "last minute panic monthly rent letter" which generally turns up on or the day before the quarter day claiming that the economy is to blame for the tenant's intention to breach the terms of its quarterly lease, and pay only one month instead of three. The payback for this breach is apparently the landlord's knowledge that the tenant is managing its cash flow more effectively and that it will consequently be a much better "partner". Incidentally I had never heard a tenant refer to a landlord as a "partner" before the credit crunch, and only then when requesting a concession of some kind. There may be Credit Managers who experience a warm fuzzy feeling when their tenants or customers are diverting payments which are properly due in order to pay other suppliers, but I must confess that I am not one of them. If a tenant wishes to vary its lease terms, then let's go back to the beginning and discuss all the obligations under the lease if it suits us to do so – and if it doesn't, then I'm afraid it doesn't, and that's the end of the conversation.

Let's be clear about this – the lease was agreed by the landlord and the tenant, probably with the endorsement of their legal representatives, in good faith, and signed in ink. Any subsequent variation needs to be with the agreement of both parties, and there should be no stigma attached to either one requiring the other to fulfil its responsibilities and keep to the contract.

When to agree and not to agree

There are however some instances where it is prudent to grant a temporary or permanent concession, and allow a tenant to pay monthly on a quarterly lease. I should stress that in each case the landlords' right to quarterly income should be maintained by either being documented in a side letter, or by not documenting the arrangement at all (the latter is only appropriate for short term arrangements as if monthly payments become established over a year or more then it could be argued that the lease has been permanently varied by consent). This way the monthly arrangement can be made conditional on the tenant's payment performance, and a default period built in which removes the concession if the tenant is two days late with a payment for example. Sadly the "give them an inch" proverb applies all too often in these situations as tenants misinterpret a "yes" to monthly rents as a "yes" to being paid when it's convenient for the tenant and not before. The landlord shouldn't regard monthly rents as the answer to all the tenant's ills either, as more often than not the payments will just have to be chased three times in a quarter rather than once. The reason a tenant asks for monthly rents is because other suppliers are twisting the knife, and there isn't enough money to go round. This means that regardless of the reason, the tenant's cash planning has not worked, so don't assume that the other suppliers will back off as a result of a landlord's concession.

At this point we come back to our covenant evaluation procedures, and look closely at the overall financial performance of the tenant company, as well as the individual performance of the unit in question. Paradoxically we are looking for something which seems to be a contradiction in itself – something which I call manageable distress. If things were going well, the tenant wouldn't be asking for concessions (and any variation to the lease terms which impacts the landlord is a concession remember), or would they?

When to say "no"

Many times I have found that a tenant which is applying for a concession is simultaneously stripping out money from the business either in dividend payments to the directors, in management charges to a group company, or even worse – spending a fortune on a store opening program which will not only benefit the tenant, but other competing landlords as well.

It is not the landlord's job to subsidise any of these activities.

It's therefore important for the landlord to satisfy itself that the distress communicated by the tenant is both a) genuine, and b) that it can be permanently remedied by the proposal on the table.

Being naturally suspicious I would also have a look at the tenant's debt structure before agreeing to anything, as suppliers of capital are still suppliers, and the landlord shouldn't be subsidising timely payments to any of them by taking a hit on the frequency of its own income. On receipt of any kind of concession application one of my first questions is "who else is being compromised to help the tenant out of a hole?" and if the answer is nobody, then it's a very short and forthright conversation.

As I've mentioned before, there is still the view adopted by some tenants that landlords are not businesses which supply space in exchange for money, but rather benevolent uncles joined to their tenants by the heartstrings, who also have an emotional obligation to ensure that their counterparties under the lease are profitable even to the extent of underwriting their losses.

By now you should know what I think of that.

A lease or any other kind of tenancy is a business transaction, with obligations on both sides. So if one side asks for a favour, there should be a corresponding compromise the other way as well. If monthly rents are requested, and the financial checks endorse their suitability in managing a short term problem, then the landlord should be looking for advantages as well. Is there a rent review pending which the landlord would like to see resolved in its favour? Is the tenant company part of a larger group which could provide a guarantee to de risk the situation for the landlord? Does the landlord want to increase its ability to manage the distressed tenant's exit from the centre by way of a landlord only break clause? All these things are up for discussion as soon as the tenant asks for something that the landlord is not obliged to give.

When to say "yes"

The economic downturn in the late noughties caught a lot of people by surprise, particularly those whose funding relied on Icelandic banks. This was a significant problem for retailers, many of whom fell into this category. The insolvency of the lenders meant that affected companies found that their over-draft facilities had evaporated overnight, meaning that as a rental quarter day approached, they simply did not have access to enough money to pay the landlords in full - or at all in some cases.

Notwithstanding my cynical comments earlier on about the use of landlords as a source of free working capital by badly run tenants, in exceptional situations like this it is only sensible for landlords to engage and assist tenants in getting through a critical situation; provided that is they are not taking unnecessary risks themselves.

In this type of situation, allowing a tenant to pay monthly instead of quarterly will smooth the tenant's outgoings and prevent it from being declared insolvent through no fault of its own. The secret here is full disclosure by the tenant of all relevant information, including corporate and management accounts, debt structure, and a forecast of how the monthly arrangement will fix the problem. If it doesn't and there are other variables involved, then by agreeing to it the landlord is foregoing two months income it would otherwise have had, without having any guarantee that the tenant will not fall into an insolvency regime anyway. Remember the landlord isn't legally obliged to do anything at all, and at the time of the crunch some of the biggest commercial companies (including my own) had to resort to multi million pound rights issues in order to avoid their own banking covenant breaches, but in the exceptional circumstances everybody faced, a few monthly rent concessions (and there weren't actually that many) was a small price to pay to keep otherwise well run tenants afloat.

Of course the inevitable happened and the standard monthly rent application letters citing "economic conditions" began to turn up on landlords' doorsteps up and down the country, without any financial information to back up the requests. Many of these were actually sent without the tenants' knowledge by their Property Agents as a way of earning a bit of extra commission. The standard answer to all these applications was the usual request for financial disclosure in order to prove manageable distress, and funnily enough most of them fell away at that point.

There will always be circumstances where a landlord will look favourably on a tenant's request to modify the terms of the lease (and in particular the payment frequency) in exchange for something the landlord wants or needs, but as we'll see when we come onto other types of concession, it's important to remember that the tenant in question is often only one of many, and any off lease deal you do with one operator will inevitably be viewed as favouritism by the others, so the effect on the mood of the entire centre needs to be taken into account. Where I've seen monthly rents given to one tenant in the past, I've soon heard grumblings from the surrounding operators along the lines of "why is the landlord helping this badly run tenant to compete on prejudicial terms with well-run operators like us?" And they are absolutely right to ask.

Start practicing your answers now if you plan to go down this route.

Rent Phasing

In situations where a tenant has requested monthly rents but where the landlord considers the credit risk to be too great, an alternative system of rent phasing is becoming more and more popular. This requires the tenant to continue to pay quarterly, but not on the usual quarter days.

In this way a tenant can reschedule rental payments across its portfolio in order to even out its cash flow, by paying landlord A one month ahead of the standard quarter day, landlord B on the quarter day, Landlord C one month after and so on. My own preference is for the tenant to pay one month ahead of the quarter day, set up in the following example:-

The tenant applies for a monthly payment concession in April to take effect from the June quarter day, but the increased credit risk of only receiving one month's rent in June instead of three is not attractive to the landlord given the tenant's covenant strength. The June quarter charges are raised in the usual way, but the tenant only pays two months, leaving a month outstanding. One month before the September quarter day, the tenant pays three months' rent in the usual way, and carries on doing so until the end of the lease, when it will need to pay the month it missed at the beginning of the arrangement. Let's be clear that this is still a concession, but with this system there are benefits for the landlord as well as the tenant.

Landlords benefit because after the initial quarter, the tenant is always making payments one month ahead of the market, and even though there is always one month outstanding, on each subsequent quarter day the landlord will already have two months' rent in hand, when under a standard monthly rent concession he will have nothing, and be chasing the first month from the new quarter.

The trigger for a large number of insolvencies is the approach of a rental quarter day which the tenant cannot meet, with the appointment of administrators falling just before the quarter day as a result, so you can see that landlords with rent phasing agreements have been able to steal the march on both their competitors and other creditors by entering into such an arrangement.

Ideally the arrangement should not be documented, as this allows the landlord to instigate recovery procedures under CRAR or the Courts (see the section "Debt Recovery") for the outstanding month's rent if it looks like the tenant is about to fail. Where it gets complicated is if the arrangement is expected to last more than a year, as the tenant can then claim – with some justification – that the phasing agreement constitutes a permanent variation of the lease terms. I suggest therefore that these arrangements are only used where the remaining term of the lease is relatively short in order to avoid a permanent compromise.

Tenants benefit in three ways. Firstly they get to reduce their outgoings for the first month of the arrangement by only paying two months out of three, improving their cash flow as a result. Secondly by paying ahead of the usual quarter day, cash flow continues to be smoothed for the foreseeable future, and by negotiating staged quarterly rent phasing payments with more than one landlord (with different payment dates), the effect on cash flow can be evened out across the tenant's property portfolio, without the additional administrative burden of paying every landlord every month. Thirdly, this arrangement can be agreed for long time periods (notwithstanding my comment about lease variation), thereby avoiding the need to reapply to the landlord every six months or so as a standard monthly payment concession expires.

A final caveat – no agreement should be entered into by the landlord before the standard covenant evaluation of the tenant company has been carried out, and the credit risk is considered acceptable.

Negotiations

When not to engage at all

Good relationships are often regarded as the be all and end all of running a successful business.

I disagree – but I expect you knew I would if you've made it to this section.

Distance is equally important.

Silence and lack of engagement is ironically a powerful negotiating tool, as it completely denies the other party a platform on which to state its case. Where there is an opportunity to gain a positive advantage most of us will not hesitate – all we need is a channel through which to do it. Now if we assume that the deal we originally did with the tenant in question is the one we wanted to do, then it's unlikely that we will want to change the terms in the tenant's favour without getting something back in return. So notwithstanding the responsibilities all landlords have regarding good estate management, there is no reason to make it any easier than necessary for tenants to raise grievances, because if they can, then they surely will. This doesn't mean that the landlord should adopt a policy of no communication at all, and there will always be situations when a problem has to be worked out by both parties, but there are other circumstances when any kind of response from the landlord will embolden unscrupulous tenants and encourage them to demand concessions which otherwise would never have been requested. Situations where silence is a good strategic tool could be when a landlord is faced with a request to modify payment terms, reduce rents, provide a rental holidays, or anything else which is detrimental to the landlord's business model. The old phrase "I'm not even going to dignify that question with a response" covers the line of thinking perfectly and sends the right signal to everyone involved.

Case Study 1

Longer ago than I care to remember at the beginning of my career, I worked for a property management company which looked after many of the large Regency blocks of flats in Chelsea. The company was catastrophically disorganised but then so were many of the tenants – particularly the theatricals and those with an artistic bent. A lot of these old buildings had centrally supplied facilities which included the heating systems. Now the invoices for the fuel oil for the huge boilers in the basements were payable 24 hours after issue, and if they weren't then supplies were automatically stopped. These invoices were pink in colour and as soon as one arrived the company would suddenly become uncharacteristically efficient. The bill would be walked round the building to the relevant people whose signatures were obtained as a priority. The payment would then be made the same day accompanied by sighs of relief from everyone involved. No communications regarding payment dates or terms of supply would be responded to, but technical issues to do with the physical supply of the oil were dealt with immediately.

Silence in this instance was the overwhelming weapon in getting the other party to honour its contractual obligations. The oil company was totally professional but expected nothing less than full compliance with the agreed contract terms, and provided the same level of service to its customers in return.

Clearly one can only adopt a payment policy like this if one is dominant in the marketplace and there are no alternative sources of supply, but isn't that exactly the position a landlord occupies with its tenants?

Even when there have been two way negotiations there is still a place for silence, as it puts down a marker that the discussion is over, leaving the recipient effectively powerless to influence proceedings any further, and totally vulnerable to punitive and unpredictable action by the silent party. I'm a great believer in saying nothing and letting the other side stew for a bit, with paranoia setting in as a result. This is a quick and simple way of removing the axis of control from the other party and establishing it firmly with the landlord. Any further negotiations which do occur will then be on a very different footing, and subject to the landlord's magnanimity and indulgence.

Case study 2

Tenant A has five trading units, each with a different landlord. The tenant has cultivated friendly relationships with four of these landlords, but the fifth is more distant and acts very much like the oil company in the previous case study. The cordiality or otherwise of the landlord and tenant relationships makes little difference during the good times, except maybe for a few more corporate jollies for the Asset Managers of the four "friendly" landlords.

Where the tone of the relationship makes a huge difference is when times get tough, and a tenant is looking for favours from its suppliers. Which landlords will it contact for a rent concession? It may still approach the fifth landlord, but it will concentrate on the other four, not really expecting a reply from number five. When the fifth landlord fails to respond it will not be seen as an imposition, but if any of the other four act the same way it certainly will. Relationships with landlords one to four will then be irreversibly damaged, while the relationship with number five will either be unaffected, or - ironically, improved.

Which landlord would you, as a Credit Manager, want to be?

Remember that schoolteachers have had all this covered for thousands of years; they know that if you go in hard and then occasionally relax the regulations it's seen by the pupils as a concession, but if you go in soft and then try to tighten things up, it's seen as an unjustified imposition. So my advice is to set your stall out early on by insisting on strict compliance with all the lease obligations, thereby ensuring that any future negotiations or variations are completely under your control and on your preferred terms.

Buffers & barriers

We can use barriers to communication strategically as well. The public sector spend vast amounts of money and time providing their customers with avenues through which they can renegotiate payment terms in the mistaken belief that this will help ensure a steady flow of income and few, if any, bad debts. This is madness in my opinion, as anyone seeking to maximise their financial position will promptly jump up onto any platform available which makes it easier for him to do so. Far better to make it difficult for would be avoiders to sidestep their obligations.

The difficulty emerges where there is genuine hardship caused by unforeseen circumstances, but these cases will be few and far between compared to the majority of cash strapped people who are simply living beyond their means. If that sounds hard then I'm afraid it's too bad, because since television found its way into our homes we have been bombarded with visions of cars, clothes, food, holidays and lifestyles as a whole which we cannot afford but which everybody else apparently can.

There's nothing wrong with trying to better yourself or give your children the very best you can afford, but the trouble starts when we give them the very best that we can't afford. I don't blame the advertising companies alone for this, and I don't see a quick fix either, it's just a fact of life that the temptation to live beyond our financial capabilities can be overwhelming, particularly if it looks like everybody else has more than we do even though we work every bit as hard.

An ideal setup therefore is where there is no direct line to the Credit Manager, as this will deter lazy people from going any further with their attempts to borrow money from their landlords. If a problem - and this applies to anything – reaches the Credit Manager it should be serious by then. Most situations should already be covered by the systems and corporate procedures we've discussed so far, all of which can be pointed out to the tenant by the rest of the credit team. This way only the critical issues need to be referred through to the Credit Manager, allowing him to spend his time doing what he's paid to do, and in the odd case where an individual does try and go over the other team members' heads, the Credit Manager will be able to ask why, and refer the applicant back to the aforementioned procedures. That will usually be the end of the matter, as a consistent response tends to deter even the most opportunistic of individuals, particularly when they can say to their own boss that "I went right to the top but got the same answer".

Good manners

If this all sounds a bit arrogant and dismissive it isn't meant to be, it's just the natural skill set and mentality which a successful Credit Manager needs to adopt up in order to protect his company, and his own sanity, from the relentless and repeated attempts by some tenants in the portfolio to undermine, sidestep, or avoid altogether the obligations they have signed up to.

However – and this is a huge however – don't ever make the mistake of letting this necessary attitude show in your dealings with your tenants, either face to face or in correspondence.

Courtesy is everything, and will provide a civilised backdrop for what might turn out to be a highly confrontational encounter. Anybody can put their point across bluntly and rudely, the true art is to be able to do it without offending, antagonising, or upsetting anyone else. If you can walk away from a meeting having given the other side the impression that you are being incredibly reasonable by not reacting more strongly to their position, and making them feel they are being unreasonable in asking for a concession, then so much the better.

This isn't just a cynical exercise in tactics of course - it's also basic good manners and the way professional people should behave towards each other.

Furthermore, remaining calm when confronted with Mr Angry is by far the best way to keep control of the situation and get your position across effectively. I accept that there will always be cases where forbearance is no longer a virtue, and where somebody needs to be deposited into the real world with a resounding bump, but losing one's own temper is never the answer – far better to simply terminate the meeting and ask the other party to leave. This draws the line in the sand just as effectively as a heated argument.

If you ever find yourself getting into a situation where your counterparty thinks his integrity, honesty, or business acumen is being questioned and begins to bristle, I find a good way of sidestepping an argument is to throw in a statement that we as landlords are only doing what we are doing, in order to protect ourselves against things that can happen in spite of everybody's best intentions. It's also important to emphasise that the tenant is being treated in exactly the same way as all the others, and is not being unfairly prejudiced.

Every now and then a member of another department (usually finance, as for some inexplicable reason this lot perpetually think they can do your job better than you can) asks to sit in on a meeting with a problem tenant. Once the initial pleasantries have given way to the inevitably frank and fair (but always polite) exchange of views, the new attendee is usually looking rather uncomfortable and completely out of his or her depth. Then when everything has calmed down – the necessary points having been made – the interloper is usually amazed that the meeting ended on such good terms.

"Good terms" in this instance of course means that both sides are able to continue to engage with each other in a civilised and faux friendly manner, whilst being free to mutter under their breath at the same time.

This is a perfectly satisfactory situation.

Keeping an eye

Credit agencies

In order to take efficient and timely corrective action you first need to know that a problem exists, so accurate information on the operational and financial status of counterparties is vital. However I'm still amazed at how many reputable companies neglect to monitor their customers' vital signs, thinking that once the contract is signed, everything will be fine and the money will automatically end up in the bank.

Unfortunately the real world tends to get in the way and things are rarely that simple, so regular monitoring of the customer base should be a priority. Thankfully it's not difficult to do, as all the big credit agencies provide daily real time updates on such things as credit rating changes, appointments and resignations of directors, court judgements, newly filed financials, mortgages and charges (including rent deposit deeds) and other public notice information including insolvency events such as meetings of creditors, CVAs, administrations, liquidations and dissolutions. Naturally this type of service costs money, but if it can be integrated into the standard financial analysis of each new tenant or counterparty, then the additional expenditure will be marginal, with the benefits easily outweighing the outlay.

Typically a new tenant should be placed on the monitoring system as soon as it's clear that the deal is going ahead; that way if something serious crops up before completion of the lease, it then gives the landlord time to withdraw from the deal before it's too late, and before a binding relationship is established, possibly including a capital contribution payable by the landlord to the tenant.

The credit agencies will send daily updates on each monitored tenant by e-mail, and scrutinising these should take priority over everything else on the to do list, as early action will enable a quick thinking landlord to steal a march on the competition by instigating recovery action if there are outstanding arrears, or by proactive asset management to either manage a strategic problem and / or mitigate risk.

Apart from notifications of potential or actual insolvency events, attention should be paid to the following:-

Resignations: If the directors of a company start to jump ship there is a reason. This could indicate a financial nosedive leading to the collapse of the business, or there may be a perfectly acceptable explanation such as the acquisition of the company by another – but we need to know the answer all the same, as it might lead to additional opportunity to expand the relationship.

Appointments: Less critical unless the individual taking up the directorship is a known villain, but it's always good to check the appointee's other directorships (if any), to see if a) there is any history of being involved with insolvent companies, or b) if there are any tie ups which will give a clue to the future strategy of the tenant's business.

Name changes: If a well- established tenant suddenly changes its name from the familiar branding to something totally random this could be a strategic move ahead of an insolvency event. For example Optical Express (Southern) Ltd changed its name to 123 Leeds Ltd just before it went into administration. This way the company avoids having a negative notice associated with the brand name published in the Companies Gazette, effectively concealing the insolvency of the company from the public and preserving the brand name and its associated intellectual property. It's an old trick which is still used regularly, so corporate name changes which seemingly occur for no reason should be treated with extreme suspicion. Once again if there is a reasonable explanation so much the better, but you still need to know what lies behind the change.

Court Judgements – the level of importance attached to a CCJ (County Court Judgement) is directly proportionate to the size of the company, and that of the judgement itself. A £125.00 judgement against a major retailer isn't necessarily a big issue as it could just be that the tenant's purchase ledger department was either asleep at the wheel or on holiday, and a bill didn't get paid when it should have been. However half a dozen judgements in quick succession should raise an eyebrow regardless of their size, as it could be evidence that the tenant is overtrading or suffering from a cash flow problem.

Big judgements on the other hand are serious regardless of whether the tenant is a household name or not, and could be due to a key supplier not having been paid, or a problem with the local rating authority.

At this point you may have to deal with well-meaning but misguided and naive members of the asset management or leasing teams, who will propose payment concessions or extensions to help the tenant get through "this difficult period". I'll cover concessions in detail later on but such suggestions should be robustly resisted, as the other creditors with judgements in their favour are in control in these situations, and they will not act in the interests of the landlord. We can therefore either voluntarily give our shareholders' rent money to these other creditors by way of a concession, or get in quick to collect any arrears ourselves by using the legal remedies available to landlords such as CRAR (Commercial Rent Arrears Recovery) which I'll come onto again later as well.

If it sounds like I'm promoting a feeding frenzy once a tenant starts to go off the rails then I'm afraid that's probably the case, because once other creditors start to take recovery proceedings there are only two results available to the landlord – getting paid or not getting paid, and the landlords' shareholders will have a clear preference, as will the bank.

Centre management

By centre management I mean on or off site Building Managers, providers of utilities such as cleaning and hygiene, security services or anybody who has a regular or periodic requirement to physically visit the trading unit that the landlord is concerned about.

These entities can provide a valuable indicator of how things really are on the ground by reporting back to the landlord any changes in the daily operation of a tenant's unit, including, but not limited to, the following:-

Staff changes such as a new unit manager.
Fewer staff in the unit than previously.
Miserable staff (or more miserable than usual).
A reduction in stock levels.
Old stock not being sold or replaced.
A lack of attention to shop window displays.
General untidiness.
Refuse build up in the unit.
Reduced opening / trading hours.
Staff complaints (such as not having been paid).
Complaints about the tenant from other occupiers.

Any of the above can indicate a downturn in the tenant's business and combined with corporate data obtained from the credit agencies, this information can provide the landlord with an early warning of an insolvency situation and / or a vacant unit.

It's not always a negative result however, as corporate and empirical date can provide conflicting results. For example, if a monitoring notice arrives one morning claiming that tenant X has new and significant court judgements against it, leading to a drastic reduction in its credit rating, enquiries should immediately be made to the onsite teams to see if anything looks amiss. If trading data is supplied under the lease then the landlord has an additional bit of information to throw into the mix, but even if not, the site team should know how well the unit is trading. If the unit is well presented, full of customers, and well-staffed, this should give the landlord some comfort. In such a case even if the tenant company should unfortunately fall into administration, there is a good chance that this particular unit will be one the administrator chooses to keep trading, and one which will be included as desirable part of a going concern sale to a buyer of the business further down the road.

A good Building or Property Manager will be in regular contact with the tenants in his or her centre(s) as a matter of course, and just like the milkman used to be, he or she is often the first to find out that something is wrong. The Credit Manager therefore needs to establish a collaborative and co-operative relationship with the people actually running the buildings, as they are a vitally important part of the credit management process – even if they don't know it themselves.

Collection Strategy

The Credit Controllers' curse.

From the first time someone was employed by someone else to collect money that hadn't been paid when it should, a curse was placed on the person chasing the debt which roughly says "you will only survive in this position if you work miracles, but at the same time upset absolutely no one either inside or outside our organisation".

That's an easy one then.

Absolutely nothing has changed throughout the years, and this was highlighted to me by a call I received from a Credit Manager after an article I had written highlighting this point appeared in one of the credit magazines. He thanked me for going into print on the subject, as he had just been able to show the article to his Sales Director, who had spent that morning on the golf course with the company's worst payer, and who currently owed a small fortune in arrears. The result of the game isn't recorded, but I'm fairly sure it involved another large order being placed by the Sales Director's best friend, and that the outstanding account wasn't mentioned.

We've already discussed at some length the different (and understandable) agendas adopted by the various sections of any business, and the pressure that needs to applied by the credit team to prevent self-absorbed sales or leasing people doing daft deals with the wrong customers. However it's worth underlining here a fundamental mistake that businesses make when balancing commercial relationships with unpaid bills:-

In cases where money remains unpaid in breach of contract terms, and where a credit professional is being prevented from taking action on relationship grounds, the company is trying to maintain a relationship which the customer has already broken. There are no shades of grey attached to this analogy – it's a black and white situation, so there's no point in interpreting it in any other way.

In most cases it is the supplier who has control over the customer, as he controls the release of goods according to his own timetables and preferences, so why the majority of suppliers are terrified of upsetting their bad customers I do not know. Perhaps it's because the whole idea of money is traditionally regarded as undignified by the British, and situations where bills aren't paid and where somebody has to point it out are outside of a lot of peoples' comfort zones – predictably leading to nervousness and emotion.

Most professional credit people don't think like this of course, as they are able to make unemotional decisions in a purely business-like manner. They know full well that the customer will be aware that he is getting away with something he shouldn't, and probably hoping that he'll get away with it for the maximum amount of time, before the supplier's credit department manages to overrule the customer's best mate on their sales team.

It's not rocket science (which I assume must be complicated, never having been involved with it), but allowing customers time to pay their bills is a kindness, and the least a customer can do in return is honour his part of the deal. The fact that credit terms are the way of the world does not diminish this basic fact one iota.

Autonomy, motivation and position

Credit control people are like musicians at a wedding – nobody wants them around until they are needed, then when it's necessary for them to perform they are expected to do so with efficiency, a minimum of fuss, and critically without upstaging the key players. As soon as their set is over they are required to disappear as quickly as possible.

Bitter? Not personally but I'm sure a lot of us are, because the responsibility resting on the shoulders of the credit controller is often unappreciated and under-supported for the structural reasons I mentioned at the start of this tome.

Indeed, as Head of Credit Control for a major commercial landlord and developer for many years I have seen evidence of this short sighted view of the Credit Professional's contribution and status on numerous occasions when dealing with new business partners and service companies.

Picture the scenario where a landlord has acquired a new commercial property, or portfolio of properties. Often there will have been an incumbent management team in place provided by one of the national managing agents, and in the short term at least it's always a good idea to keep them in place, as they know the history of the property, the tenant relationships, and where the bodies are buried.

The agent's management team arrive at the landlord's head office for a meet and greet session with the key instructors from their new landlord client – including yours truly. There will be the Head of Finance, the Property Managers, the CEO perhaps, the Head of Sustainability (no I don't know either), and a few accounting people. When asked (by me) where the credit control team are I receive the predictable response from the Head of Finance "oh if you've got any problems just let me know and I'll get so and so to look into it for you".

Oh dear.

This is where things have to change, and I ask for a face to face meeting with the credit team, as they will be reporting directly to me, and not going through Superiors or Surveyors (via the wine bar – sorry that was unkind) in order to communicate time critical information to the Head of Credit Control within their client, and get an immediate instruction as to how to proceed.

There have to be checks and balances of course, so if recovery action is required and the agent's Credit Controller asks me for permission to take it. He or she has an obligation to inform the team at that end about what is happening, and similarly it's my responsibility to inform the property team on my side. This isn't because either party needs the authority to take whatever action is necessary – that should be a given; no it's actually a practical measure to ensure that all elements of the situation have been taken into consideration. For example there may be a large amount outstanding from a tenant which is not responding to the usual chasers, causing the Credit Controller to ask me to authorise CRAR or another form of recovery action. However what if there is a delicate and confidential relocation or exit being negotiated which will be completely scuppered by intervention from the credit team? That's why all recovery workflows must ensure that ongoing commercial discussions and sensitivities are considered – even if they are not important enough to prevent the action.

Once again it's important to point out that the definition of "commercial sensitivity" does not include the unwillingness of Leasing Executives to upset anyone they deal with on a regular basis.

So, we've established the reporting lines to and from the managing agent's credit team and their new client, and immediately given the agent another problem.

If we assume that the cleaners occupy position 1 on the managing agent's corporate totem pole and the CEO occupies position 10, then the Credit Controllers will fit into the structure at perhaps point 4 (some are probably thinking "it's actually point minus 1" right now), and salaried accordingly. However I need them to occupy a higher position within the hierarchy to take account of the authority and responsibility balance (each needs the other in order to function efficiently) that doing the job properly requires.

There's no quick answer to this, so it's a question of ongoing demonstrations of how well the procedures can work, thereby educating the agent's management team in the benefits to be gained from letting their professional credit team have sufficient authority and responsibility to provide the required level of service to their client. This will allow the agent to more easily achieve its cash collection targets and reduce the client's bad debt provision accordingly.

Sooner or later the "I told you so" scenario I mentioned earlier on will crop up and the credit team will have established themselves as key players in the agent's relationship with a valued client - and that's exactly how it should be.

Creative Thinking

A good Credit Manager will soon build up a mental picture of the portfolio of tenants and / or customers he oversees, and can sometimes act as an intermediary to fix strategic problems which threaten one entity, by putting one party in touch with another. He can also act as an advisor or massage credit terms to get round a cash flow problem. Here are a few quick case studies from my own personal experience:-

Example No 1 - An overstretched customer:

I worked for many years in the telecommunications industry where my company supplied the green phone cards which were once so prevalent, along with payphones and associated technology to payphone management companies in the UK and abroad (a business which has now been all but killed off by mobile phones). I had one customer who I knew had taken on a competitor's portfolio, and who was now struggling with the management, overtrading wildly, and letting things generally get out of control. I was concerned that the business would run out of ready money to honour its day to day obligations and end up in administration before very long.

I also knew of another customer from a different region who was keen to expand as he had nationwide maintenance arrangements, spare capacity, and enough cash to finance not only an acquisition, but the running costs thereafter. I spoke to both principals and suggested a way around the problem - it was a bit touchy politically, as these individuals were competitors in the same marketplace, but ultimately a sale of part of the distressed company's portfolio was completed to the company with the spare capacity. The benefit to my company was that all the existing arrears from company number one were paid as part of the deal, and we ended up with two solvent and operationally stable companies to sell to whereas before there had only been one.

Example 2 - Short term cash-flow issues.

I once took on a new position within a large supply company where my remit was the usual "do whatever you need to do to sort out the mess" (with the unspoken subtext "but don't upset the customers" of course). The company's financial exposure to its customer base hadn't seemingly been controlled in any way, and there was a lot to do if we were to regain control of the income stream and avoid extensive write-offs. One of the largest problems was a significant debt owed by a major customer which had got itself into day to day cash-flow problems even though on paper the company had plenty of assets. The dilemma was how to ensure that the customer had sufficient stock to keep trading and avoid legal action from other suppliers or HMRC, without allowing my own company to get in any deeper. I sat down with the senior management of the customer company and looked at a) their ongoing contracts with their own customers, b) their requirements for stock, and c) their obligations to other suppliers. We then worked out a solution by simply manipulating the credit limit and payment terms. It transpired that a couple of months down the line there was a two month window where the customer's own supply contracts dropped to a lower level, so we used this as a vehicle to reduce the credit limit to 50% of the current (and historically wildly exceeded) one, so that during this period no further stock would be supplied until further credit headroom was created as they settled the outstanding debt under an agreed schedule. Once more stock could be supplied under the new lower limit I would allow 60 days payment terms instead of the usual 30 days – this allowed the customer to pay off even more of my company's debt as money from their own customers came in (they were required to maintain and enforce their own 30 days supplier payment terms).

So by simple strategic and temporary changes to credit terms we helped a customer continue to trade efficiently without holding up supplies to its own customers, while at the same time clearing its debt to us. I also went from having a large arrear on 30 days payment terms which could never have been collected, to an arrear of under half the size on 60 days terms which was well within the means of the customer, and which was paid exactly on schedule.

I should add that this type of arrangement can only be used if the customer company is fundamentally solvent, and only experiencing working capital problems – if this is hadn't been the case I'd have been first in line with a Statutory Demand.

Example 3 – Assisting with finance

I'm including this little story as a point of interest rather than as tactical advice, but it does show that anything is possible if one looks beyond the immediate players in any scenario and considers their relationships with other parties who might currently be out of sight.

Some years ago a large national chain went into administration, and only a small number of the retail units (all very large and typically in retail parks) were taken on by the new owners of the business. This left the administrators with a number of unwanted properties which they were keen to offload to anybody who would take them. The problem was that the units in question were old and dilapidated, and nobody was prepared to invest the money to upgrade these "sprinkler free rat holes" (their words not mine) and turn them into useable trading units. Finally a buyer came forward who was prepared take on the leases and undertake this work, but only if the existing landlords (and there were numerous) would grant a 3 month rent free period following the assignment to cover the cost. This seemed unlikely as each landlord would have its own financial issues and banking covenants, so there seemed to be a stalemate. I was approached by the potential buyer to see if I could offer any advice, and my suggestion was that they speak to each landlord and offer an extension on the lease post-assignment in exchange for the rent free period. This would allow the landlords to go to their own banks (who would be expecting to see regular rental payments) and agree a three month payment holiday in exchange for a prolonged period of occupancy and a stable income stream.

I'm pleased to say that this suggestion was taken up by the buyers and in the case of most of the leases it was very successful.

Concession Applications

Some of the following points were touched on in the section on monthly rents, which are also a concession, but here we'll go into more detail and cover all forms of rental concession, as the rules are basically the same.

I'm constantly amazed by the lack of understanding that a commercial landlord is not only a business with its own targets to meet, but that it can often be an investment platform for other institutions as well. The big landlords are a popular destination for investments from financial institutions such as global pension funds, banks, trusts, and other vehicles, and without exception these investors need to see a return on their money otherwise they will pretty quickly move it somewhere else.

It's easy therefore to see how a run of concessions or rental holidays which weren't included in the landlord's business plan can cause a significant reduction in the forecasted income (and therefore the valuation) of a commercial property, and seriously reduce or wipe out any growth in value for the pension fund which has lent the landlord its money.

Ironically such a situation will impact upon the pension outlook for the tenants as well, as the amount of money in their personal funds will not have grown as forecasted, and at the end of the day their pension payments will be lower. The worst case scenario is where a high profile pension fund investor sells its shares in the landlord, causing other investors to follow suit in a chain reaction which continues until the landlord goes bust, the former investors have all lost a fortune, and nobody is looking forward to a happy retirement.

This is why rent concessions need to be granted in exceptional circumstances, only where there is clear financial evidence of manageable distress, and conditional on some form of benefit for the landlord – a "what's in it for us?" argument.

I'm going to confine this section to rental concessions requested for financial or trading reasons – there will always be situations where a lease has come to an end, or a tenant has exercised a break notice, and the Asset Manager will negotiate a rent reduction in order to keep the tenant in the premises until an alternative occupier can be found to pay the full rent. These situations are part and parcel of everyday asset management, and whilst they are technically concessions they do not establish a negative precedent, as a) other tenants will not be in the same position to seek favours, and b) they do not reduce forecasted income for the landlord, and so can be treated quite differently.

There seems to be a misguided perception in some sections of the business community that the landlord has a duty to underwrite a tenant's losses, and that a commercial tenancy agreement obliges the landlord to ensure that the tenant's business thrives whatever the cost. The fact that there are plenty of businesses out there run by people who haven't a clue doesn't seem to matter, nor does the aforementioned point that the landlord's primary motivation is to make a profit for itself and its investors.

For this reason some tenants when faced with a cash flow or debt repayment problem or a lack of income caused by poor sales, will approach the landlord before they even speak to their own bank.

This is not a good situation for the landlord, but it represents a huge win for the tenant if the landlord simply rolls over and reduces the rent, as it's simply free money. If the tenant were to go to its own bank or investors for the funding they will eventually have to pay it back with interest, so the "landlord bank of first refusal" suddenly becomes very attractive.

We therefore need to find a way of separating the genuine cases of manageable distress with attempts to capitalise the tenant's business at the landlord's expense.

An absolute precondition for any application for a rent concession must be the provision of up to date management accounts for both the unit in question, and the tenant's business as a whole. If this information isn't forthcoming, then it's impossible to decide whether a concession is justified or appropriate in the circumstances.

There's a bit of a conflict here, as apart from things like signage and trading practices which are contained in the lease and which apply to all tenants in the building or centre, the landlord has no control over the way the tenant conducts its business. The disconnect between the parties is extremely valuable in situations when things aren't going well, as the landlord (who suddenly starts being referred to as a "partner" by the tenant) is not obliged to intervene at all, but can insist on additional financial information on a regular basis in exchange for assistance.

A lot of this will depend on the landlord's corporate attitude towards the tenants in its property portfolio – some have a much softer approach than others, and this is usually due to the type of property concerned and its status within the marketplace. It's much easier to ignore a tenant's requests for financial assistance in a super prime centre where other tenants are cueing up to replace him, but in a secondary property where there are already a couple of void units the landlord will naturally need to adopt a more conciliatory approach.

Either way it's up to the landlord to maximise any available benefit and minimise losses for himself and his investors – anything else is pure negligence.

Is a rent concession the answer?

I'm not for one minute suggesting that rental concessions are never justified – we'll come onto a couple of examples where they were, but the decision to grant one or not should be made from a position of knowledge, not of conjecture, and if a concession is the best solution to a critical situation, it should be obvious for all to see, and significantly outweigh other alternatives.

Giving your customers money without obtaining any benefit in return is not generally regarded as good business practice, yet many landlords seem to do just that. Throwing cash at a problem by way of a rent reduction or holiday solves nothing in the long term, and accepting the tenant's justification for the concession at face value is simply asking to be taken advantage of. If things are going wrong it's a good idea to do some research and find out what's really happening, and this should include an analysis of the tenant's corporate financials, up to date trading figures for the unit in isolation and the company as a whole, along with empirical information from the landlord's Property or Centre Manager, who should have a pretty good idea of the situation on the ground and be able to make recommendations of his own.

To state the blindingly obvious, we need to understand the root cause of the problem, and whether it's confined to the unit in question or is indicative of a general decline in the tenant's business. The usual suspects are as follows:-

Poor sales

If the trading accounts for the unit show a decline in turnover which is not reflected in the trading accounts for the overall company, then it means that the tenant's overall management or debt structure is not the issue, and a local solution is required. This is good news for the landlord, as it means that the problem is solvable and he won't have to stand and watch helplessly as his tenant goes bust anyway regardless of any assistance he is prepared to give.

Staff

The Centre Manager is a vital part of the landlord's team as he or she will have been speaking to the tenants on a regular basis, and will know if there are issues involving staff attitude, churn, discipline and attendance, or simply whether they make interacting with customers a pleasant experience or not. If things were going well until the new shop manager took over, then it's not hard to pinpoint the problem and feed it back to the management. In such a situation there is no justification for any assistance from the landlord, as it's not his job to subsidise the negative effect of inadequate management or poor staffing by the tenant. But if the unit in question is adequately staffed by motivated individuals who greet customers with a smile but avoid pestering the life out of them (the best way of driving a Brit out of a shop – please take note Mr Retailer), then the poor sales performance must be due to something else.

Stock & pricing

If customers don't buy what's on offer, it's because they don't want to. That's a simple fact that many businesses seem to struggle with. The reasons for not wanting to are equally simple - is the item offered for sale:-

1. Too expensive?
2. Too cheaply made for the price (not the same as too expensive)?
3. Available nearby?

4. Available online?
5. An unknown brand (is it any good and will it last)?
6. New to the market (is it any good and worth the money)?
7. Badly packaged or presented (try selling pink spanners and see how far you get)?
8. Something nobody wants anyway (e.g. Sinclair C5 for those of you who are old enough to remember).

If any of the above applies, there is little the landlord can do to improve things, so giving free money by way of a rent concession is simply throwing it down the drain.

Adjacency

This cuts both ways as another retail tenant offering the same service or product will naturally cannibalise sales from both outlets, however you regularly see similar types of tenant such as mobile phone operators or fashion chains concentrated in the same area in a shopping centre, and we're all used to seeing Currys and PC World next to each other in retail parks. The argument in favour of this is that customers will go to the centre or retail park because they know they can compare products and prices easily, otherwise they might not bother at all, so in reality the positives probably cancel out the negatives.

So for a tenant to request a rent concession due to being out-performed by a nearby competitor is a bit rich as long as all other things are equal, however if the landlord has just installed a major chain operator (with its inherent economies of scale) right next door to a local independent, causing an immediate drop off in his sales, then clearly the local operator has a bit more of a case.

The landlord's decision to either grant or refuse a concession in these circumstances is probably going to be influenced by the level of guilt or sympathy he may or may not feel for the applicant, and how much he may consider he has contributed to the tenant's poor trading.

There is another point about adjacency which is often overlooked as well, and that is when a concession has been requested and deemed appropriate. This means one operator is trading on preferential terms in the midst of other well run and financially stable competitors, who will feel justifiably aggrieved whether they are in the same retail sector or not (we touched on this in the section on monthly rents as well).

Even if a concession is subject to a confidentiality clause involving the most painful of consequences for the tenant if he breaches it, the other tenants in the surrounding area will still find out – it's just a fact. The landlord therefore needs to balance up the negative impact of having one struggling tenant who hates him for not granting a rent concession, against a larger group of good tenants who hate him just as much for doing so.

The wrong location

This one comes up periodically, and whilst location (and access to footfall) is important to all sorts of businesses, we have to remember that the tenant entered into the letting agreement for the premises in question with his eyes wide open, and presumably having carried out his own due diligence. Now if the landlord has subsequently built an escalator right outside the tenant's shop front, or altered the configuration of the building in a way that undermines the tenant's presence, then there is a conversation to be had, but if nothing has changed since lease commencement, then there is no obligation for the landlord to compensate the tenant for his poor choice of location - even if it was the only site available. Once again we need to remember that it is not for the landlord to run the tenant's business at any point, particularly if he is only being invited to "contribute" now that things are not going as well as everybody hoped.

It goes without saying that Asset Managers and Leasing Executives are paid to anticipate problems like this and avoid installing tenants in questionable units – the good ones do just that. However if the building has changed hands and the tenancy has been acquired from previous owners, you may well find yourself in this sort of situation. It's therefore important to include an assessment of tenants' trading performance when undertaking due diligence on any potential acquisition.

Seasonality

This is not just about confectioners doing well at Easter and card shops doing well at Christmas. There are distinct patterns affecting tenants which recur year on year, and which have a bearing on their ability to honour financial commitments. As I've mentioned before, the lure of a rent concession is hard to resist when a company is struggling and doesn't really want to admit it to the bank or other stakeholders, and the temptation to use the landlord's rent money to pay other creditors is ever present. This needs to be seen for what it is - bad cash management - and resisted accordingly.

If we take the traditional quarter days we can see different ways in which an undercapitalised tenant will feel pressurized at different times in the year:

The March 25th quarter day comes after two months of generally slow post-Christmas trading, and this coincides with payment due dates for trade suppliers who provided Christmas stock on 30, 60, or 90 days' credit. The tenant will want to discharge the trade suppliers' debts first as a) they won't get any summer season stock until they do, b) because low liabilities look good on year end accounts, and c) because there may well be an upper limit on creditor balances imposed by the bank as a condition of granting a business loan. The March quarter day is therefore "last minute panic monthly rent application letter" time, even though everyone but the tenant can see the squeeze coming miles away. Once again it's not the job of the landlord to provide free bridging loans.

The 24th June quarter day is in my experience not overly troublesome, as good weather and long days help maintain demand for goods and services offered by most tenants in retail centres. The exceptions are the greeting card retailers who have a long wait before the next seasonal spike in their revenue streams.

The 29th September quarter day is the start of the Festive Season for many retailers, as they will be buying in Christmas stock from this point onwards, and need to clear down their credit accounts with the wholesalers. The trade suppliers' Credit Controllers know this of course and will insist that everything outstanding is paid off so that they can maximise new orders without increasing the retailer's credit limit above that recommended by the credit rating agencies. Once again there is a huge incentive for a retail tenant to try to "rob Peter to pay Paul" and use the landlord's rent money to service other debts.

The 25th December quarter day is boom time for retailers apart from those selling big ticket items such as cars, washing machines and carpets. Concession requests will therefore come from this section of the market which does indeed suffer from a drop in demand at this time of year. However once again this should have been foreseen by any decent management team as it happens every year, and unless there are unit specific issues such as those already covered, the remedy lies in a conversation between the tenant and his bank manager, not with the landlord.

There are of course businesses which are overtly seasonal – bicycles sell well in the summer and toboggans sell well in winter, so if a tenant is firmly established selling one or the other, and has no way or smoothing out its annual income, then the landlord can, and often will, help.

This does not however require a rent concession (i.e. a reduction), but a stepped or irregular rent, with more payable in the good part of the year than in the bad. Ideally such an arrangement should be factored into the original letting deal, so everybody knows what to expect from the outset, and the cash flow problem is prevented from occurring in the first place.

Market trends

I find that retailers are generally very good at analysing market trends, but rather poor at reacting positively to them, and the number of high profile companies who fail because nobody wants their stuff anymore bears this out. The big example of course is technology – physical games and CDs have been in terminal decline for years due to online competition, but the same old retailers kept selling the same old product until the inevitable happened and they collapsed. We all have 20/20 hindsight but if the consumer could see that the CD had become a niche market item rather than a mainstream one, then why couldn't the people selling them? The tyranny of the status quo plays a part in this, as does gambler's ruin – "if I keep going just that little bit longer everything will be fine". It's either basic human nature or sheer folly, but either way totally understandable if you've got nowhere else to go.

Rent concessions then are a) a favour granted by the landlord, b) going to cost the landlord money he will never get back, c) a source of intense irritation to the other tenants in a property, d) not likely to address any long terms issues at all, and therefore e) best avoided except in exceptional circumstances.

Debt Recovery

CRAR

I've already mentioned the statutory regime entitled Commercial Rent Arrears Recovery (CRAR) pursuant to The Tribunals Courts and Enforcement Act 2007 in the section under leases, and even though it's nowhere near as useful to landlords as its predecessor the Common Law of Distress, it's still an additional remedy landlords can employ which is not available to other classes of creditor.

It should be remembered however that CRAR can only be invoked to collect pure rent, and not other charges which may or may not be reserved as rent under the lease. This includes service charges, insurance, water charges, and rates, none of which are collectable using this mechanism.

CRAR came into force on 6th April 2014 to a fanfare of disgust from the landlord community, which had only been "consulted" after the Bill received Royal assent and became an Act in 2007. The punitive elements were therefore already set in stone, and what consultation there was only related to housekeeping issues.

Distress (i.e. the use of Bailiffs) to seize goods and chattels from a premises in lieu of rental payments has often been seen as an unfair advantage in favour of landlords by other creditors, but the point most of them miss it that it compensates the landlord for its inability to terminate the supply of its product, namely trading space. Everybody else – including utility companies-can simply withhold further deliveries until such time as the arrears have been settled. Landlords cannot do this, even if the tenant enters into an insolvency regime and continues to use the premises.

CRAR can be instigated as soon as 7 days' worth of rent has fallen due and not been paid, and this means the day after the due date for weekly, monthly, quarterly, and annual rents payable in advance. The Enforcement Agents (formerly known as Bailiffs) will send a CRAR letter (which is a prescribed notice) to the tenant which includes an additional fixed fee of £75.00 representing the Agent's charges for carrying out the service.

Now once the letter has been delivered, and this can be by e-mail, the following clause in The Tribunals Courts and Enforcement Act 2007 comes into force:-

(1) For the purposes of any enforcement power, the property in all goods of the debtor, except goods that are exempt goods for the purposes of this Schedule or are protected under any other enactment, becomes bound in accordance with this paragraph.

Now then, not many people know that.

It is therefore the case (and The Ministry of Justice alerted me to this), that once the letter has been delivered, all goods remaining in the unit are effectively the property of the landlord until such time as the rent has been fully settled. It's arguable how powerful this clause is, as no one to my knowledge has either absconded with the stock, or gone into administration and legally challenged the strength of the binding. However as with all untested clauses, its power lies in its role as a deterrent, in this case discouraging tenants or subsequently appointed Administrators and Liquidators from disposing of the stock without accounting to the landlord first.

If no payment is received for seven days after the CRAR letter has been delivered, it is then up to the landlord to decide whether to a) seize and remove the stock from the unit, or b) enter into a Controlled Goods Order. Seizure is usually only carried out when there is no other choice and the tenant is about to abscond or go bust, the thinking being that the available options are either some money from an auction sale or nothing at all.

As we've discussed before, there are those in the tenant community who see landlords as a source of free finance, to be utilised at their discretion by using the landlord's properly due and payable rent money to pay other suppliers. Clearly this isn't an acceptable situation so a Controlled Goods Order can be the best solution. In a way it's just a formal extension of the binding arrangement, whereby the Enforcement Agent takes a full inventory of the stock in the unit, charging the tenant 7.5% of the arrears for the privilege. This additional charge can be a deterrent in itself, so it's important to tell the tenant in advance if you're going to do this, as payment often arrives pretty quickly afterwards.

Once the Controlled Goods Order is in place, the Enforcement Officer can pursue the bound goods if they are removed by the tenant and physically reclaim them from another property, rather than it being a compensation situation if goods are removed when only bound by a CRAR letter.

One upside to the new regulations is that whereas many landlords would refrain from sending physical bailiffs to attend the unit of a major, but delinquent retailer, for fear of damaging the relationship (that word again, and remember the retailer has already broken the contract), they will happily send CRAR letters. So the big tenant companies are no longer protected from recovery action by their presence and influence in the market place, and we'll all drink to that (except the tenants in question of course).

If seizing and removing is the only action likely to resolve a situation where a tenant simply will not pay, then the goods can be disposed of in one of two ways:-

Removal by the Enforcement Officers to a vacant unit nearby, under the control of the landlord.

This gives the landlord the option of auctioning the stock on the open market from the premises without incurring storage charges, or more significantly, to sell the stock back to the tenant in exchange for payment of the arrears.

Removal by the Enforcement Officers to an auction house for storage and sale.

This is a last resort option as there are significant fees to be paid before the landlord sees any proceeds, including valuation fees, auctioneer's fees, storage fees, and the Enforcement Officer's additional fee of 7.5% of the realised value. This is on top of the 7.5% he has already charged the tenant for the seizure and removal. As a result the amount of money ultimately available to the landlord us often pitifully small, and the decision to use this remedy is often one of principle rather than expected financial recovery.

Offset, coercion and outright blackmail

Where a tenant exists in more than one unit it's clearly sensible to manage the accounts harmoniously, in other words to view the tenant's arrears position globally, so if the tenant is chasing for a refund of a credit balance on one unit while still leaving charges unpaid on another, it is basic common sense to either offset one account against the other and pay back the balance, or simply refuse to pay anything until the arrears are settled. This can be complicated if the properties are held by different subsidiary companies and / or joint ventures, but it's clearly worth doing in order to protect the landlord's position. Where third party collection or managing agents are involved and financial security needs to be maintained because of sensitivity, the Credit Manager will need to be the intermediary, ensuring that everything is clear on all other properties before physically refunding any money.

The same principle can be applied to lease negotiations or discussions concerning rental concessions, as these all represent situations where the tenant wants something which the landlord is not obliged to give. These situations are therefore the perfect opportunity for the landlord to clear up any existing issues with the tenant as part of a portfolio wide settlement. Visibility of arrears across all the tenant's properties is therefore very important, particularly as property companies usually manage their portfolios by individual centre due to the different ownerships and joint ventures in which they are often held.

Litigation

County Court actions

Following the abolition of the Common Law of Distress and the introduction of CRAR (see the section CRAR") it is no longer possible to take control of a tenant's goods in lieu of unpaid service charges, insurance, or anything not described in the lease as principal rent. Indeed the proportion of service charges contained in an all-inclusive rent has also to be deducted from an action under CRAR.

Therefore the only (legal) way to recover service charges from a trading tenant is via the Courts, and in most cases the amount outstanding will dictate that a County Court claim is the most appropriate method, with High Court enforcement further down the line if necessary.

The same process will need to be used where a tenant has absconded from a property while still owing the landlord money, or (heaven forbid, but it's happened to me) where a well-meaning but naive and misguided Surveyor has allowed (without the authority to do so) a former tenant to pay historic arrears in instalments, which then fail to materialise.

Any half decent Credit Controller knows how to sue people – let's face it it's one of the more dynamic and satisfying parts of the job - but it's not always cost effective to take individual actions using the national firms of high profile lawyers that many property companies retain.

The more proactive firms of Enforcement Agents (remember we're not allowed to call them Bailiffs anymore) have therefore come up with an integrated recovery model to collect all the landlords' due income in one go, using CRAR for the rent and a simultaneous County Court claim unless the service charge is paid as well. The service charge element has been referred to as SCAR (service charge arrears recovery) which most of us find rather amusing and entirely appropriate. This process means the landlord only has to give one recovery instruction, and does not have to involve its own expensive lawyers. The enforcement firm will make a profit either from a commission or by retaining the interest on the collected debt, but either way the landlord should receive most, if not all, of its money.

Statutory Demands

For larger debts where CRAR or SCAR is not appropriate (for example where the seized contents of a premises will not cover the amount due), the landlord can instruct its lawyers to issue a Statutory Demand. This formal notice will give the recipient 21 days to either dispute the debt or pay up, failing which a Winding up or Bankruptcy Petition can then be issued depending on whether the debtor is a company or an individual. The trick here is to make sure that there is no possibility of the defendant arguing that there is a dispute concerning the debt, as the Court will not engage in the process unless the full amount in question is fair and due. The Court will not examine the evidence to see if a genuine dispute exists, they will simply throw the Statutory Demand out, leaving the landlord with an unrecoverable bill for its legal fees. In circumstances where there is a contentious element to the debt due, it is sometimes a good idea limit the amount claimed under a Statutory Demand to a lesser figure which cannot be disputed, in order to get the process underway.

Statutory Demands are most effective when used strategically, in other words where a tenant knows that its entire business is at risk from a Winding up Petition if it doesn't pay the debt within the 21 day gestation period. Ignoring the action and paying the landlord at the last minute won't help much either, because a Winding up Petition will be advertised in the Companies House Gazette for all to see.

Winding up Petitions

The filing of a Winding up Petition can have a disastrous effect on the tenant company, as the credit rating agencies will immediately circulate the Petition to their subscribers (remember those daily monitoring notices), who will in turn take action on any arrears they have with the company, or refuse further supply. Lastly and most damagingly of all, the suppliers credit insurers may pull cover and that's generally the final straw.

Most intelligent management teams will know how dangerous a Statutory Demand can be, and will engage with the landlord immediately to limit the damage – if they don't then the chances are their company is on the slide anyway and having a Statutory Demand in place is a good position for the landlord to be in anyway.

Bankruptcy Petitions

Rightly or wrongly there is still a stigma about being made bankrupt, as in contrast to corporate insolvency, an individual can't claim that he was a victim of other peoples' incompetence, and has to bear full responsibility for getting himself in to this unenviable situation. To those around him (family, social circle, golf club, former suppliers and customers etc.) he will be seen as either foolish or dishonest, and will do all he can to avoid this stain on his character and reputation. A Bankruptcy Petition therefore is another valuable tool in bringing a defaulting individual or proprietorship under control, and once again if things have already gone too far, then the serving of the Petition would have been the right action to take anyway.

Insolvency

Administration versus Liquidation

These two insolvency regimes are often confused but for a landlord the primary differences can be summed up as follow:

In an administration neither the Administrator / tenant nor the landlord can bring a lease to an end without either the leave of the Court or the consent of the other party.

In a liquidation both the Liquidator / tenant and the landlord can bring the lease to an end as they see fit, and there are several mechanisms available to achieve this.

So you can see that the system is balanced and actually works quite well, although of course there are some complications.

Administration

Let's take administration first. There are two types – the traditional administration sometimes known as a "post pack" and a "pre pack" administration.

A "post pack" is where a company runs into difficulties and for a number of reasons cannot afford to pay its debts as and when they fall due. An Administrator can be appointed by a charge holder (usually a bank), a creditor, or by the directors of the company themselves. The immediate effect of this is the imposition of a legal moratorium on recovery action from creditors, and any legal actions already underway are stayed.

It's worth pointing out at this stage that an administration order cannot override any terms in the lease other than the requirement to pay rent (and then only if the unit is not trading – but we'll come to that), so lease terminations, conditional surrenders, break clauses, and compliance issues such as quiet enjoyment and waste disposal are all unaffected and enforceable in the usual way.

Having sat down in the CEO's chair (and a lot of CEO's don't understand that they become surplus to requirements at that very instant), the Administrator will attempt to find a buyer for the good bits of the business and obtain the best price available. He does this for two reasons – firstly as his duty as a Court appointed officer is to produce the best result for all the creditors, and secondly because he is a commercial business as well and needs to see his fees for the job paid in full.

Following a period of marketing, during which the Administrator may well run the business in order to keep the staff in place and honour existing customer and suppliers contracts (although suppliers will only be paid for post administration orders), a sale of the assets will hopefully be completed. This will either be to an existing company or to a new company formed to take over the business. Either way the landlord will at this point be approached to assign any leases which the new version of the tenant wishes to retain, to the new company.

These applications to assign can be treated in exactly the same way as any others, with no obligation on the landlord to give consent, although as usual it is not to be unreasonably refused. The standard evaluation of the assignee's creditworthiness should be carried out, and if the proposed assignee fails the covenant criteria – perhaps because it is a new start-up company (possibly formed by some of the failed company's directors who have raised enough money to buy back the business), then the landlord can ask for the usual safeguards such a rent deposit or personal guarantees as a condition of the assignment.

Sadly in many cases the landlord doesn't have an alternative tenant lined up and the administration will result in a vacated (but not surrendered) unit unless he agrees to the assignment, so the ability to dictate terms will be severely limited. Market forces prevail in these situations, and Administrators will usually try to arrive at a solution which is acceptable to both sides, however it's much easier to come to a satisfactory arrangement if there are more than one of the insolvent company's units in the landlord's portfolio. A deal can then be done which keeps all the landlord's units open and trading in exchange for some rental concessions, which in turn can necessitate the landlord being granted a rolling break in the lease. Once again the rent concession mentality comes into play where the landlord needs to be able to replace the existing (and subsidised) tenant with another, if the new one will pay the full rent.

A "pre-pack" administration is where all the marketing, packaging and sale of the business has been agreed in advance of the administrator being appointed. The sale of the assets of the business to the new owners then occurs contemporaneously with his appointment, effectively presenting creditors with a fait accompli. Pre-packs sometimes generate negative comments in the press particularly where members of the insolvent company's management team have formed a new company and purchased a streamlined version of the business, leaving underperforming leases, bad business decisions, and crucially the old company's creditors behind. They are not all like this of course, and for niche businesses where there are only a few players in the market, they are a valuable way of rescuing a business without either damaging its reputation via a long winded and public marketing campaign, or losing key employees who may not sit around until a "post-pack" sale has been agreed. Once the Administrator has sold the assets of the business to the buyer, either in a "post-pack" or "pre-pack" deal, the implications for landlords are identical, and applications to assign the leases can all be treated the same way.

The role of letting agents

I previously spoke about Letting Agents in the section under tone and evidence, but it's worth mentioning their role in the insolvency process as well, as it's not necessarily a welcome one.

Historically when a tenant went into administration the landlord would be visited by the new buyer of the business and a representative from the Administrators to discuss arrangements for the continued occupation of the insolvent former tenant's units.

However these days Administrators tend to drop out of the picture (even though the moratorium protecting the insolvent company from legal action remains in place), once the sale of the assets of the business has been completed. The meeting with the landlords is now usually attended by the new owner of the business (who might bear an uncanny resemblance to the old owner of the business) and his highly incentivised Letting Agent. Neither of these individuals are remotely interested in doing the best deal for the company's creditors, as that obligation rests with the Administrator. No, our friendly neighbourhood Letting Agent is purely interested in getting the best deal for his client – the new buyer of the business, and reducing fixed costs (aka rents) to the lowest level possible to generate additional downstream profit. He will of course be paid a commission on any reduction he can obtain.

Personally I think that the Administrator should be present during all negotiations with landlords to stress test any proposals, and confirm that unit X really does trade poorly and requires a rent reduction, and that the Letting Agent and his client aren't trying to pull a fast one.

I've raised this numerous times with members of the insolvency profession, and the official answer is always "well the terms covering the sale of the assets of the business are confidential", which I think is a bit pathetic, as the relevant parts of the sale and purchase agreement (i.e. the classification of the leases) could easily be disclosed to the landlord subject to a signed confidentiality agreement.

The real reason for all this secrecy of course is that the buyer and his agent don't want the landlord to know important the property in question is, as they want to get the lowest rent possible regardless of whether it's justified or not.

Liquidation

In a liquidation, there is no likelihood of a going concern sale, and the Liquidator's job is to realise the best value he can from a piecemeal sale of the company's assets. Now in many cases one of the principal assets of an insolvent company is the property it trades from, because it owns either the freehold or an ongoing lease. There may of course be an extensive property portfolio if the business was large enough, but either way the Liquidator will look at these assets not as component parts of the business as a whole, but as individual pieces of real estate.

Any insolvency practitioner's ultimate obligation (apart from getting his own fees paid of course) is to realise the maximum amount of money for the company's creditors, and he doesn't have to take into account the landlord's interests. He can therefore apply to assign the remaining period of a lease to a third party (in exchange for a premium payable by that third party into the liquidation coffers), leaving the landlord having to justify any refusal to give consent to the assignment. Such consent is always "not to be unreasonably refused", so the landlord can find himself on his back foot very easily when faced with a proposed assignment to a new tenant which doesn't stand up on covenant or tenant mix grounds.

The saving grace for landlords in these situations is the ability that both parties have within the liquidation process to bring a tenancy to an end without the consent of the other.

A landlord faced with an undesirable assignment can make the problem disappear on one of two ways:

1. Forfeiture by means of peaceable re-entry. This is Surveyor language for simply changing the locks and taking back control of the unit. As with any formally documented forfeiture, the lease is brought to an end and the landlord is liable for business rates from that point onwards. Similarly a liquidated former tenant has the same right to apply for relief from forfeiture (i.e. to have the lease reinstated) as a live one, so the landlord needs to bear in mind that for six months after the date of forfeiture this is a possibility.

   Frankly given that the former tenant ended up in liquidation, probably leaving unpaid rent due to the landlord which would have to be paid as part of a successful application, the likelihood of this happening is minimal, and in all my years in property I have never seen an example. In fact I have overseen the peaceable re-entry of numerous units from liquidated companies, in order to re let them immediately to new tenants without any problems at all.

   A new tenant will naturally seek reassurance that its newly fitted out and established trading unit will not be snatched away without compensation, following a successful application for relief from forfeiture; this can be achieved by the landlord giving the new tenant an indemnity against such an eventuality for the 6 month application window. This indemnity costs the landlord nothing, and allows the new tenant to invest in staff, marketing, and fit out without worry, and even though an application for relief is theoretically possible, it's unlikely to happen, and even less likely to be successful.

2. Notice of Election. This is a legal application by the landlord for the Liquidator to formally disclaim the lease, bringing it to an end. Normally the liquidator will issue a disclaimer as soon as the property in question is of no further use in order to place the rating burden back on the landlord, but the Notice of Election gives the liquidator seven days in which to either issue the disclaimer or provide a good reason (good in this instance means it will stand up in Court) not to. If no disclaimer is issued and the landlord proceeds with Court action, the Liquidator will automatically be faced with a costs order in favour of the landlord if the landlord wins. The procedure is similar to the Civil Procedure Rules Part 36 application, and I'm surprised that it isn't used more regularly as it is a powerful tool.

3. Disclaimer. As noted above, this is a legal mechanism whereby a lease is brought to an end, and is only available to Liquidators, The Official Receiver or a Trustee in Bankruptcy. There are no terms to be negotiated, and all obligations relating to occupancy the property which previously were the responsibility of the leaseholder now revert to the landlord, including the payment of business rates.

The CVA

CVAs or Company Voluntary Arrangements have been in and out of the news over the last 10 years or so, as this form of corporate "rescue" is often employed by large retail companies who have got themselves into difficulties, but who also consider the underlying business to be sound. Simply put, a CVA is an agreement between a distressed company and its creditors, overseen by an Insolvency Practitioner (known as the CVA Supervisor), which modifies the contractual obligations of the company. The proposal for the agreement is put to a vote, and if 75% of unsecured creditors and 50% of unconnected creditors (i.e. no intercompany creditors) vote in favour then the CVA terms are legally binding on all creditors of the company from the start date set out in the proposal.

However CVAs are sometimes seen as a strategic mechanism to undo bad business decisions and allow the same management to keep trading in better terms than before, so it's worth setting out the arguments for and against this controversial restructuring tool:-

An instrument of rescue or restructure?

As a form of corporate rescue for companies in genuine distress, I think most landlords accept that a CVA is better for them in certain situations than administration or liquidation. However it shouldn't be forgotten that CVAs are also better in the short term for the CVA Company itself for the following reasons;

1. A bespoke remedy: A CVA by definition is created on behalf of the distressed company, and is therefore formulated to be of most benefit to that company - not its creditors. An administration or liquidation is a rigid, non-negotiable regime imposed on the company from outside, and is designed to maximise the return for all creditors equally subject to their ranking status.

2. No Required Changes to Management Structure: A CVA allows the existing company to continue trading under the same management, whereas an administration requires the business to be sold to a new company, even if it is controlled by the same management. Administration allows third parties to bid for the business as a going concern, and could theoretically lead to a better return for the creditors than under a CVA.

3. No Assignments of Leases: A CVA does not require ongoing leases to be assigned as there is no change to the identity of the tenant. This has benefits for landlords in terms of reducing tenant changes in shopping centres for example, but it also leads to a significant saving in legal fees for multi occupancy tenants such as retail chains, and is a big advantage for them over administration.

4. A Targeted Compromise: The big retail CVAs since the credit crunch have compromised specific creditor groups (usually landlords in order to maximise the future financial return for the company), whilst leaving other creditors, such as trade suppliers, largely unaffected. An administration compromises all parties including trade suppliers and capital, including Directors' shareholdings.

So who really benefits from a CVA?

In a CVA all creditors have a vote based on their exposure to the company, but all can be outvoted and bound by a majority vote from other creditors who might not be as severely compromised under the CVA. The voting formulae used in some CVAs have attempted to give landlords a share of the vote proportionate to their losses, however this only underlines the fact that they are losing more than other creditors and is entirely right. Compromised creditors do have the opportunity to request modifications to the CVA terms, but any concessions are usually minimal and unlikely to offset the prejudicial effect of the CVA on their businesses.

Having said all this, CVAs are usually marketed as a lesser evil to administration or liquidation, and often contain benefits such as an obligation to meet business rates on closed units for a fixed period or until termination. This is an undeniable benefit for landlords.

CVAs are too often adopted as a condition of future investment in a company by third party financiers. It could therefore be argued that, as well as being a vehicle for rescuing a distressed business, the CVA is also a mechanism to legally strip out underperforming assets with none of the disruption or stigma that accompanies an administration, in order to benefit the company, its investors and / or shareholders in the future.

This all leads some credit professionals to hold a rather jaded view that a CVA can be used as a handy get out of jail free card to give inefficient management another bite at the cherry.

Furthermore, the fact that a number of big retail CVAs in the past have ultimately failed to save the businesses from administration leads us to a rather obvious question – does a CVA merely delay the inevitable? The failure of the BHS CVA would suggest so, but I think it's fair to say the jury is still out. It is however a fact that many creditors see a CVA as an orderly wind down rather than a rescue operation.

Given current economic uncertainties, it is likely that we will see more CVAs in the future. Finding an appropriate middle ground lies in engagement between stakeholders and the insolvency community and strong dialogue; something that the various trade bodies have tried hard to establish. However, in terms of the shape of future restructuring proposals, the insolvency profession holds the cards.

It must of course be remembered that with all insolvencies there is a certain amount of pain to be shared, and most creditors accept this, however there is a feeling amongst landlords that this pain could, and should, be shared more equally amongst creditor groups.

For example I strongly believe that Insolvency Practitioners need to have a better understanding of landlords' business models and investment structures, and need to avoid the easy option of driving down rents and pulling out of marginal units whilst leaving other creditors largely unaffected. As I've said in previous sections, Landlords are businesses which are reliant on income from let properties and any CVA proposal that provides flexibility in managing their assets will be seen more favourably than those that don't. For example, proposals that provide the option for properties to be taken back by landlords should a new letting proposition arise, that include an element of empty rates mitigation, and include a gradual programme of closures, are measures that landlords will look more favourably on.

Some CVAs have included a market cap compensation fund which undertakes to repay money to compromised creditors (usually landlords) if the CVA company goes on to exceed trading expectations. This is a welcome step in the right direction, and mechanisms like this which allow compromised landlords to share in the upside of a successful CVA should certainly be included in future CVA proposals. However I'm not aware of any situations where any creditors have seen a penny so far.

For creditors to support CVAs they need to a) be convinced of the viability of the distressed company's core business and its place in the market, b) be convinced of the capabilities of the management team, and c) understand the recovery strategy for the business going forward.

Being fair for a minute, the CVA landscape has seen a lot of changes and activity over the last few years, and a lot of good work has been done in to increase transparency and fairness, but it needs to continue so that creditors and in particular land-lords can feel that the CVA supervisor is an ally in a critical situation, rather than someone working purely to get a better deal for his own client. It's up to you to decide where you sit in this ongoing debate.

Powerhouse

Finally in this diatribe about the pros and cons of the CVA, I must mention the highly controversial case which started the row in the first place and which galvanised the creditor (i.e. landlord) community to resist CVAs which were clearly detrimental to their businesses. In 2007 a white goods retailer called Powerhouse proposed a CVA which called for rent reductions across its store portfolio. Nothing unusual about that – but what it also did was to remove payment guarantees which existed on certain of the leases from Powerhouse's parent company the Pacific Retail Group (PRG) registered in New Zealand. This meant that where before if Powerhouse had gone bust the landlords could approach PRG for the rent under the guarantee, now they could not, leaving PRG free and clear of its former obligations.

This didn't go down too well with the affected parties.

As a result a group of landlords mounted a class action in the UK High Court to overturn the CVA (it had been voted through by other creditors who weren't nearly as badly compromised) on the grounds of unfair prejudice, and they won. The resulting judgement stated that a CVA <u>can</u> strip out a parental guarantee <u>provided</u> the bearers of the guarantee are equitably compensated – in other words if they are given something else of equal value. This was not the case with Powerhouse so the parent company PRG ultimately had to pay up. The first thing I look for in a new CVA proposal is any hint of guarantee stripping, and I suggest that everyone else does the same, as having learned nothing from Powerhouse another retail chain Miss Sixty tried the same thing shortly afterwards, and this CVA was similarly overturned citing the Powerhouse judgement.

Personal Insolvency – IVAs and Bankruptcy

The IVA

The IVA or Individual Voluntary Arrangement is predictably the baby brother of the CVA, and shares much of its structure, but this time relating to an insolvent individual rather than a company. Usually an IVA is proposed as a result of one of the individual's creditors getting too close on his or her heels, and is an attempt to avoid the stigma of Bankruptcy. This way an insolvent individual can dictate the terms of a proposed settlement with his or her creditors and stipulate how much of the monthly income will be allocated to the IVA creditors. The IVA is voted on in the same way as a CVA but in reality there is usually one overriding creditor who can swing the vote one way or the other. IVAs also have a reputation for a) going on for far longer than the stipulated period (usually 2 years), b) being modified as time goes on and as the insolvent individual omits to honour his or her obligations, and c) never paying creditors the promised amounts. If an individual who owes you proposes an IVA I recommend making a full doubtful debt provision against the arrears while doing what you can to engage with the IVA supervisor (an Insolvency Practitioner) to modify the IVA terms in your favour. You probably tell that I'm not a fan of IVAs so best of luck.

Bankruptcy

Bankruptcy has more in common with liquidation than any other insolvency regime and applies to an insolvent individual rather than a company. A Trustee in Bankruptcy (again an Insolvency Practitioner) has control of the individual's assets and estate and will do what he can to maximise the disposal of these assets for the benefit of the creditors. The things to watch out for in bankruptcies (as with liquidations) are disposals of assets in the six months running up to the Bankruptcy Order, as in far too many cases the impending bankrupt will attempt to sell desirable assets (the car for example) to his or her spouse at a knock down price in order to stop the Trustee selling it off. If you suspect this has happened contact the Trustee immediately, as any reputable Insolvency Practitioner will take a very dim view of this sort of thing.

Partnership administrations

Partnership administrations are quite rare but they do occur, and are where one or more individuals have been trading under a brand or firm name and have issued invoices and maintained accounts in that name, but who have not registered it as a limited company. This allows genuine small businesses to minimise accounting overheads and start and stop seasonal businesses when the work slows down, but it also allows unscrupulous individuals to run up debts in the firm's name and then deny any involvement. Any attempt by the creditors at recovery action will probably fall on stony ground as the defendant (the firm) doesn't exist legally. For this reason one should never enter into any kind of contract with a counterparty which is not a legal entity such as a company, an individual, or a registered charity. If a partnership or firm asks for an order or a property lease it must be made out to the individual partner's names – this way the individuals are jointly and severally liable for any debts, and the seller or landlord will be able to avoid having to accept a (very small) dividend provided by a partnership administration and pursue the individuals for the full amount.

Things to watch out for

Name changes

Companies change their names for a number of reasons:

1. Branding: A company set up some time before with a generic name might subsequently have established a successful brand in the marketplace, and now wants to change the name of the company to associate itself more closely with the brand name. This makes absolute sense and is nothing to worry about from a credit perspective.

2. Dissociation: A company that has received negative press coverage for whatever reason will change its name to dissociate itself from past misdemeanours. If a name change turns up in the daily monitoring of the tenant database and there is no obvious branding issue, a closer look at what is going on is justified.

3. Insolvency: Once again if a company changes its name without there being an obvious reason why, it could be a precursor to an insolvency event. Lots of companies change their name to something strange and wonderful just before they go bust so that the original company's name, and the goodwill value of commercial brands associated with it will not appear in the Companies Gazette, thereby protecting the post insolvency value of the assets of the business. So if a name change appears on the daily monitoring, particularly if it's an established

company changing its name to something odd, then it's likely that there is an insolvency event just around the corner – so be warned, and make sure all the money's in.

Appointments & resignations

Most monitoring services run by the established credit agencies will give details of appointments and resignations of the directors of companies being monitored. A series of appointments can give comfort if there are doubts about a company's longevity, but a series of resignations – particularly if the CFO jumps ship – can be an early warning that things are not going well. Similarly if a monitoring notice flags up the appointment of a known miscreant as the director of a formerly well behaved tenant, then there could be a bumpy road ahead. These monitoring notices get you ahead of the game and are easily worth the money spent on the subscriptions – get them every day, read them, and act upon them immediately.

The Enemy Within

There comes a time in the career of every Credit Manager (actually several times in my case) when somebody at Board level asks the question "why are we spending all this money on credit control and credit reporting when we don't appear to need either?" Now I'm sure you already know the answer to this, but for some reason the basic logic that credit management exists primarily to prevent problems occurring in the first place seems to totally elude senior managers who are paid a great deal of money to know better.

This is partly due to the traditional mistaking of credit management for debt recovery (as noted in the introduction), but probably more to do with the fact that most people want to live in a pink and fluffy world where every customer is a good one, and this mind set fits in nicely with the optimistic and positive approach that salesmen and senior managers adopt for all the right reasons. Remember, if they could do without you they would – in a heartbeat – so it's not surprising that after a period of stability they all start dreaming and deluding themselves that all those dodgy customers and nasty bad debts have gone away forever, and that the Credit Manager who made it all happen is now surplus to requirements.

Sadly the better the credit team are at their jobs the easier it all looks to those with no idea. However in my experience it takes just two quarters for established procedures to unravel, and two years to put it all back together, so a smart Credit Manager will regularly point out to all and sundry that just because everything is in place today, it doesn't mean it will be tomorrow, particularly in times of economic uncertainty of the kind we've seen in recent years.

Summary

Effective credit management then, rather than just being a series of procedures, is a mind-set, and once you get used to identifying the areas of risk, it's relatively easy to come up with something simple to plug the hole. It's rather like defensive riding for cyclists – if you assume that every other road user is either clueless, blind, incompetent or just simply out to get you, you have a much better chance of survival. Some might say that the landlord's job is to help the other road users to get safely to their destinations as well, and that's not necessarily wrong, but the trick is to avoid the joyriders, drunks and kamikazes before they drag you / the landlord down into the gutter with them.

I wish you the very best of luck.

And they all lived happily ever after.

The End.

About the Author

A Member of the Chartered Institute of Credit Management, Duncan Grubb has been active in the Credit Management Industry for his entire career. After attending Colfe's Grammar School and Portsmouth Polytechnic, he spent time in the commodity trading, freight and telecommunications industries. However the majority of his work has been within the property sector, and from 2001 to 2015 he was Head of Credit for Hammerson Plc, a leading commercial landlord. From 2008 to 2015 he was also Chairman of The British Property Federation Insolvency Committee, a trade organisation which responds to government consultations, and provides a unified voice for the UK property industry.

He now runs his own company Duncan Grubb Consultants Ltd, and takes part in speaking events for trade organisations. He also contributes articles to trade publications.

He lives in South London with his wife, two Children, three motorcycles, and far too many guitars.

Website: www.duncan-grubb-consultants.com